MW01028662

Great Shall Be Your Joy

Great Shall Be Your Joy

RECEIVING THE POWER OF OUR SAVIOR'S LOVE

STEVEN A. CRAMER

International Standard Book Number
0-934126-48-8
First printing March 1984
Second Printing March 1985
Third Printing April 1988
Fourth Printing October 1989

Printed in the United States of American

Published and distributed by:

Preface

It took me over thirty years to discover and to admit that no matter how long I lived, no matter how hard I tried, I was never going to overcome my weaknesses, correct my faults, and conquer my sins by myself. It took me even longer to discover the startling truth that God never expected me to do so.

Learning how to work as partners with Christ, learning how to draw from him the grace, wisdom, and strength I needed to reach beyond my own limitations, I found the way to make him a very real part of my life. This book was conceived in that discovery.

It is an exciting adventure to learn from the scriptures, then from experience, that virtually any problem can be solved through receiving the personal assistance of our Savior Jesus Christ, who has repeatedly given the assurance, "My grace is sufficient for all men."

Introduction

> I stand all amazed at the love Jesus offers me,
> Confused at the grace that so fully he profers me. . .
> ("I Stand All Amazed," Hymns No. 80)

All my life this hymn has been one of my favorites, giving me a feeling of closeness to the Savior and prompting me to live a better life. It was not until I began this study, however, that I realized how little attention I had paid to the actual words. For years I had been singing that I was "confused at the grace" which Jesus offers, but not only was I not confused by his grace, I had scarcely given it a thought. With a shrug of piety, I had carelessly tossed the word "grace" (I didn't even know it was a doctrine) onto a spiritual "junk pile" along with the rest of my supposed "protestant theories."

Nevertheless, in due time, the Lord's grace became a major influence in my life. Indeed, it literally saved my life—both physically and spiritually. For many years I lived a life unworthy of a member of the Lord's Church. I was proud, rebellious, unclean and wicked. Eventually I was excommunicated. After many years, when I finally tried to repent of my sins, I found myself in serious trouble. I discovered that all those years of deliberate wickedness had placed me in a condition of spiritual bondage—that I was held captive by

Satan's power because of the countless times I had yielded my agency to his evil promptings. I found myself bound by the chains of evil habits and attitudes that I could no longer overcome, and I was afraid.

As I struggled to repent, I suffered intense feelings of discouragement, depression, confusion, and hopelessness. I felt so helpless that I lost all hope of ever making my life right again. Even worse, I grew weary and sick of trying. I hurt, and I resented God for causing, or allowing, my problems. I felt so ashamed of my sins and weaknesses that I hesitated to go before him in prayer. I felt lonely, unloved, unimportant, inferior, and totally unworthy. I was ready to give up. Soon most of my waking hours were spent dreaming of ways to escape, which would eventually have resulted in taking my own life.

But then came the miracle of his grace. As I proved to the Lord (and to myself) that I was sincere and committed in my desire to repent, and as I continued my struggle to free myself from the grasp of Satan's chains and from the grip of my own fears, resentments, bad habits and feelings of worthlessness, the Savior reached out with his amazing grace and touched my life. As he began to work his miracle within me, I was released! I was given freedom! He blessed me with strength where I had suffered life-long weakness. He gave me the ability to cope with circumstances and pressures which had previously dominated and overwhelmed me. He comforted me and healed my spiritual wounds. In short, he helped me face and conquer every emotion, habit, and opposition which had led to my fall, and which had conquered and enslaved me. He gave me victory.

I wish I could describe the incredulous confusion I felt as the Lord welcomed me, loaned me strength, and caused me to discover how important I was to him—sinful as I had been. I could not comprehend it as I felt him open his arms of love to me. The question I had to have answered was: "Why, after more than thirty years of trying to find him, was this happening now? What made the difference?" I cried out to Heavenly Father in my confusion, "How is it Thou wilt allow me to come to Thee? I am so unworthy. I am such a failure. How can I be acceptable to Thee? All these years—I have tried and failed so many times. Even now, as I try to repent and forsake my sins, I still cannot control my habits nor my passions. I don't know the way back to Thee. I don't understand Thy love." Soothing me much as a loving parent does a troubled child, his reply was simple. *"Trust Me, My son. You don't need understanding yet. Just allow Me to guide you, and together we will work out all the problems."*

And so, it was in giving my life over to the Lord in complete surrender that I experienced the miracles of his grace. I learned to trust him as I walked that unfamiliar path. Then, as I felt the miracle of his healing touch in my life, as I felt his power working in me, as I felt him actually changing my nature and my desires, and as I felt him replacing my bitterness and guilt with forgiveness and love, I was compelled to record what was happening to me. Hence, this book.

As I experienced the wonderful, healing influence of his divine grace, I plunged myself into a search of the scriptures to try to understand the miracle that he was working within me. Using scriptural concordances I found over two thousand references to the workings of his power and grace! (I also found that more than thirty of our hymns refer to the doctrine of grace.) As I devoured these scriptures I was dumbfounded. I was absolutely astonished by the marvelous promises these scriptures offered and which I found working in my life. He literally rescued me from the jaws of hell, and I finally did come to "stand all amazed" at his grace. I continue to stand in awe today.

While the truths I learned were new to me, I make no claim to presenting "new doctrine." The truths have always been there in the scriptures and manuals, but the spiritual blindness caused by my sin and self-sufficiency prevented me from understanding them. I do not ask anyone to accept these ideas based upon my word alone. I have tried to demonstrate the truth of every principle with scripture and quotations from Church leaders, Sunday School, Relief Society, and Priesthood manuals. More important, however, than those documentations, is the promised witness of the Holy Ghost to every person who seeks "with real intent." (Moroni 10:4-5.) It is important for each person to rely upon that witness of the truth, and also to draw upon the same inspiration as they learn how to *apply* the truth in our efforts to live the Gospel and grow closer to the Lord.

I compiled the book because a person cannot find all that I found and dare to keep it to himself. I now invite the reader to come with me through these pages of discovery. I challenge you to let go of resentments and failures long enough to explore the possibility that you, too, can find and accept the Lord's amazing grace in your own life.

Steven A. Cramer

★**Note:** All emphasized scriptures are the author's emphasis. All other italicized, quoted materials are notated in their references.

To all those who helped me turn from the pride and dark blindness of my independence and self-sufficiency into the brilliant light, freedom, and joy of victory through the grace and the merits of Jesus Christ.

The Beginning

I heard the crowd before I saw it.
As I reached the top of the hill I gasped.
Three men were hanging from crosses,
Blood flowing from their hands and feet.

The one in the center was different.
His face was also covered with blood, flowing from a crown of
thorns.
But it was his calm serenity that held my gaze.
Why wasn't he screaming in anger and pain like the other two?

His eye caught mine, and I knew this was no ordinary man.
A charge of . . . of what? Awakening? Challenge? Love?
Invitation?
Whatever it was, it flowed through me and . . .
I knew I would never be the same.

Suddenly his manner changed.
I wondered what he meant and where he got the power to shout:
"It is finished!"
Like the others, I trembled in fear as the sun grew dark and the
Earth shook beneath us—as if in angry protest.
When I looked again he was speaking softly, reverently
to someone unseen.

"Father, into thy hands I commend my spirit."
Before I could question his meaning, he smiled at us as if—
As if he were leaving—just for awhile.
He bowed his head, and I knew he was gone.
There was nothing left but the torn, empty shell. And suddenly—
I was lonely.

I turned to the man he had called John.
He was trying to comfort a sobbing woman.
"Excuse me, sir, but who was that man?"
"Come with us," he said, "and we will tell you."

The work had begun.

Steven A. Cramer

Table of Contents

I
Grace

In the preface to this book I described my discovery of God's grace. For the first forty-two years of my life, without realizing it, I shut his influence out of my life and tried to find happiness in my own way. I failed.[1] When I finally did discover the marvelous power of his grace, however, I found I had been living in spiritual poverty in the midst of abundance.

Consider the experience of someone standing in a beautiful flower garden surrounded by thousands of flowers of every color and variety, all in perfect bloom. Imagine how dull and empty that would be if the person were color-blind and had no sense of smell! That was like me. Because of my ignorance about God and his grace I had failed to obtain the joy and peace which is available to every person through him.

When I finally opened my life to the Savior, I found the abundant life he came to share with us. I found forgiveness, peace and hope. I found safety and security. I found faith, trust, and wonderful truth. But more important than all these, I found freedom and release from what I had been and

---

[1]This story is written in detail in the author's book, *The Worth Of A Soul,* A Personal Account of Excommunication and Conversion.

what I had done. I found victory over sin and Satan and myself. I found God's unconditional love for me. And, in finding all this through his grace, I also found myself. As I then studied the doctrine of grace, I found its explanation had been there in the scriptures all along, scriptures I had read many times—I had simply been blind.

Definitions

Webster defines grace as "a virtue coming from God," and as "unmerited divine assistance given man for his regeneration or sanctification" (*Webster's Seventh New Collegiate Dictionary,* Springfield, Mass.: G. & C. Merriam Co., 1963).

The Bible Dictionary which is printed in the back of LDS bibles states: "The main idea of the word [grace] is *a divine means of help or strength,* given through the bounteous mercy and love of Jesus Christ . . . It is likewise through the grace of the Lord that individuals, through faith in the atonement of Jesus Christ and repentance of their sins, *receive strength and assistance* to do good works that they otherwise would not be able to maintain if left to their own means. *This grace is an enabling power* that allows men and women to lay hold on eternal life and exaltation after they have expended their own best efforts." (Emphasis added.)

One LDS author has defined grace as "an unearned gift or endowment given as a manifestation of divine love and compassion, for which the recipient does not pay an equivalent price. But though grace is unearned, it need not be unmerited." (Hyrum L. Andrus, *God, Man And The Universe,* 1st Ed., S.L.C., Utah: Bookcraft, 1968, p. 206.)

While these three definitions are helpful, they seem incomplete. Perhaps grace can only be understood by experience. Because it is such an integral part of God's love, the doctrine of grace cannot be reduced to the confinement of mere words, but we must try.

"My Grace Is Sufficient"

In the 1974-75 Melchizedek Priesthood Manual, lesson thirteen discussed the difficulty we so often have in learning to depend upon the Savior for the strengths we lack. Subtitles in the lesson included the following:

> "Jesus Taught His Apostles To Be Dependent On Him For Their Success."
>
> "How Does The Teaching Of Man's Dependency On Christ Apply To You?"
>
> "How Does Dependency On Christ Lead To Spiritual Success?"
>
> "Is Dependence On Christ Necessary For You?"

This was a memorable lesson. At the end of the lesson the chart shown below was presented to summarize the message of the lesson material and to illustrate "the gap" which exists between our abilities and the resources required to fulfill our assignments.

"SUCCEEDING BEYOND ONE'S NATURAL ABILITY"
(DEPENDENCE UPON CHRIST)

OUR TASK

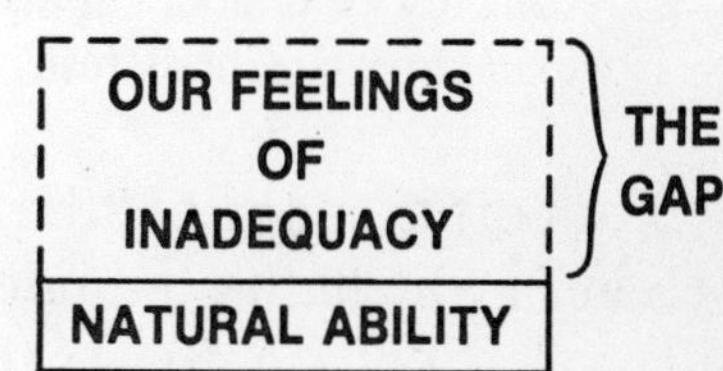

> "What would Jesus have you do to comprehend the influence of Christ's power in your life, in order that you may work out your salvation with increased humility and with a greater sense of dependence upon Him" (1974-75 Melchizedek Priesthood Manual, *When Thou Art Converted, Strengthen Thy Brethren,* p. 87)?

What does the Lord mean by his frequent assurance that "my grace is sufficient for thee"? (See D&C 17:8; Ether 12:27; 2 Cor. 12:9.) He is telling us that it does not matter how large "the gap" is which exists between our ability and the strength or wisdom required to perform a task. No matter what our need is, no matter how great our "gap" is, no matter how often our need occurs, or how complicated that need may seem to us, his grace "is sufficient" to accomplish our purpose—provided that we are sincerely willing to depend upon him to fill our gap with his grace as we continue to do all we can. The great message of Christ's feeding the multitudes with only a few loaves of bread and fishes is that we can always start right where we are by using the limited resources we do have, and then relying on him to fill the gap between our total need and our limited ability or resources.

> And God is able [if we cooperate] to make all grace abound toward you; that ye, always having all sufficiency in all things, [necessary for our growth and well-being] may abound to every good work (2 Cor. 9:8).
>
> . . . let us have grace, whereby we may serve God acceptably with reverence and godly fear (Heb. 12:28).
>
> But my God shall supply all your need according to his riches in glory by Christ Jesus (Philip. 4:19).

Paul often spoke of "the praise of the glory of his grace, wherein . . . he hath abounded toward us in all wisdom and prudence" (Eph. 1:6, 8). As the Savior's grace flows into our lives "in all wisdom and prudence," he is careful never to do anything for us that we could do for ourselves. To do so would intrude upon our agency and rob us of growth.

> . . . God . . . does not do for us one thing that we can do for ourselves, but requires of us that we do everything for ourselves that is within our power for our salvation. I think

> that is logical and reasonable. On the other hand, the Lord has done [or will do] everything for our salvation, that we could not do for ourselves . . . (Joseph Fielding Smith, *Doctrines of Salvation,* 3 Vols. compiled by Bruce R. McConkie, 6th Ed., S.L.C., Utah: Bookcraft, 1955, Vol. 2, p. 308.)

Grace, then, is God working in us to expand our own efforts as we try to reach beyond the limitations of our natural capabilities. It is a gift of power from God which enables us to achieve that which we could not have done by ourselves. (Eph. 2:8; 1 Cor. 2:12; Ether 12:8-9; 1 Cor. 1:4-5.) How wonderful it is to discover that his grace "is sufficient" to be all things to all needs. There are no boundaries or limitations. His grace, however, does not have the same effect upon every person. Because each person has different needs and abilities we read that we each receive "gifts differing according to the grace that is given to us. . ." (Rom. 12:6).

How often our children come to us for help. There is no subtlety or embarrassment in their request. "I can't tie this by myself. Will you please help me?" Or, "I have a problem, and I can't decide what to do." The Savior said that unless we adults discover our need for his help and then come to him "as a little child," we will never enter the Kingdom of Heaven. With such magnificent power available to us, why are we too proud to admit our "gaps" and ask for help?

REPRESENTS THE SIZE AND DIFFICULTY OF AN ACHIEVEMENT

WHEN WE HAVE SUFFICIENT ABILITY ON OUR OWN, WE CAN ACHIEVE IT BY OURSELVES

There are many things we can do on our own without the need for grace.

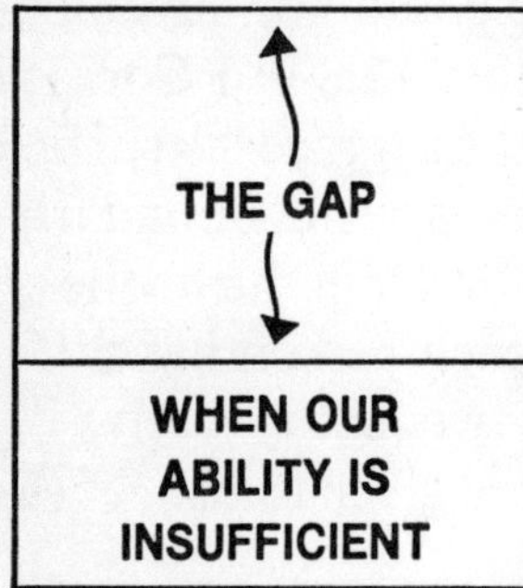

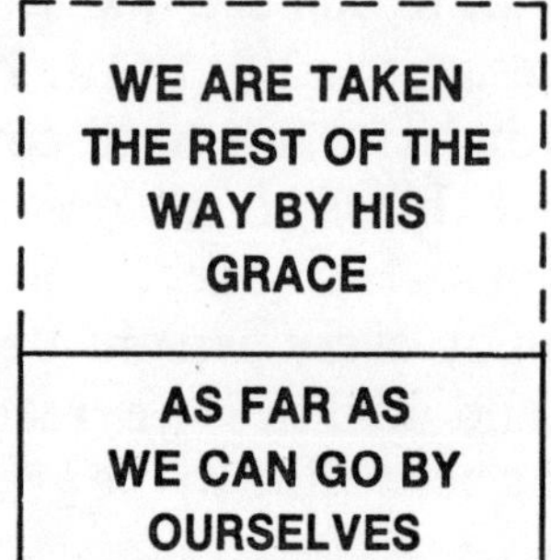

There are many tasks we cannot accomplish without help from Christ.

> Therefore, dearly beloved brethren, let us cheerfully do all things that lie in our power; and then may we stand still, with the utmost assurance, to see the salvation of God, and for his arm to be revealed (D&C 123:17).
>
> He [Jesus Christ] possesses all the attributes of the divine nature of God. He is virtuous, patient, kind, longsuffering, gentle, meek, and charitable. *If we are weak or deficient in any of these qualities, He stands willing to strengthen and compensate* ("Jesus Christ: Our Savior and Redeemer," Ezra Taft Benson, *Ensign,* November 1983, p. 8; emphasis added).

By Grace Or By Works?

In the 1975-76 Melchizedek Priesthood Manual the chart shown on the next page was presented to clarify the balance we need between faith in the grace of the Savior, and the good works of the law that we will do when we have that genuine faith.

While there are many scriptures that proclaim our salvation through the grace and atonement of Jesus Christ, there is not one verse of scripture that even hints that grace can substitute for or replace our works. The following words of Paul's are one of the most frequently misquoted verses used to teach the false doctrine that we are saved by grace alone, without the need for works.

> For by grace are ye saved through faith; and that not of yourselves: it is the gift of God:
>
> Not of works, lest any man should boast. (Eph. 2:8-9.)

In the very next verse, however, Paul emphasized the importance of righteous works, not to save us or to put God in our debt, but to make his grace possible in our lives.

> For we are his workmanship, created in Christ Jesus unto good works, *which God hath before ordained that we should walk in them* (Eph. 2:10).

When someone tries to interpret a scripture in such a way that works and grace seem to be in competition, then the interpretation is in error. We are not saved by grace instead of works! We are saved (and exalted) by the grace which is made possible to us through our works.

> Therefore ye are justified of faith and works, through grace, to the end the promise might be sure to all the seed. . . (Rom. 4:16 J.S. Translation).

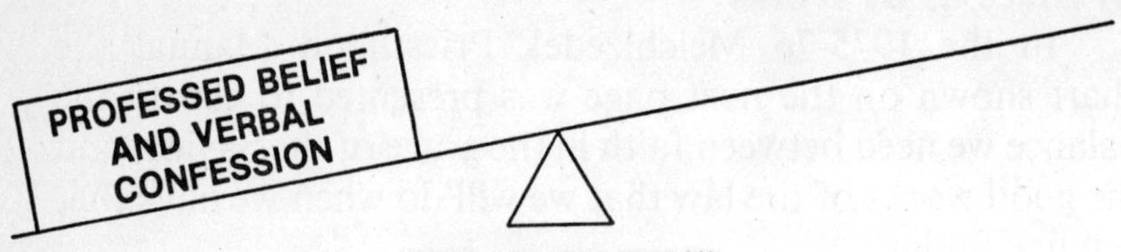

"DEAD FAITH"

"An unbalanced life exemplified by many professed followers of Christ."[2]

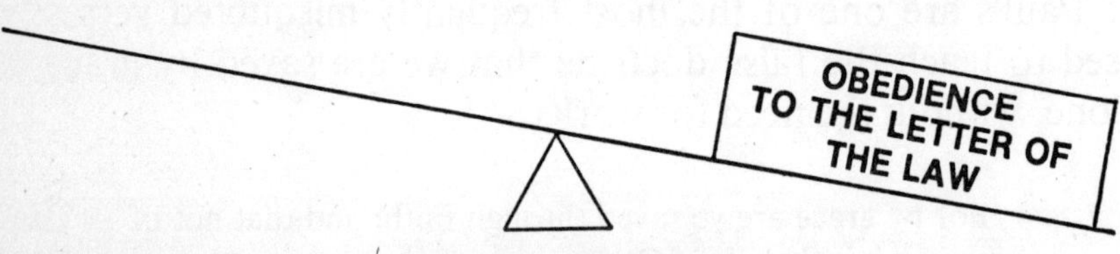

"DEAD WORKS"

"An unbalanced life exemplified by the Jews of Christ's day and by many who trust that a 'good life' is all that is required."[2]

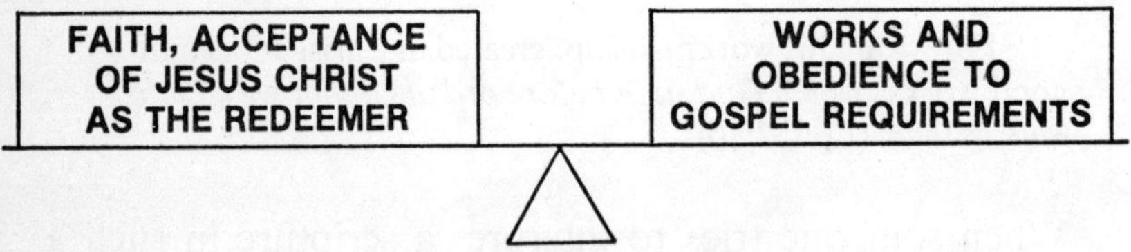

"The balanced life required for entrance into the kingdom of God."[2]

---

[2]1975-76 Melchizedek Priesthood Manual, *A Royal Priesthood,* pp. 82-83.

> And God is able to make all grace abound toward you; that ye, always having all sufficiency in all things, may abound to every good work (2 Cor. 9:8).

Our works cannot earn our way out of our accountability for our sins, but they can reconcile us to the Savior and win his approval so that he will be justified in standing as our substitute when it comes to penalties and punishment. (See 2 Ne. 10:24; 25:23; 33:9.) Before the Lord will do that for us we must prove ourselves to him by living in righteous obedience to his commandments. In other words, it is by our righteous works of obedience and service that we make it possible for the Lord to apply his grace in our behalf. It is as Paul said: ". . . even so might grace reign through righteousness unto eternal life by Jesus Christ our Lord" (Rom. 5:21). The partnership of grace and works is clarified by the principles taught in the two scriptures below:

> Therefore, dearly beloved brethren, let us cheerfully do all things that lie in our power; and then may we stand still, with the utmost assurance, to see the salvation of God, and for his arm to be revealed (D&C 123:17).
>
> For we labor diligently to write, to persuade our children, and also our brethren, to believe in Christ, and to be reconciled to God; for we know that it is by grace that we are saved, after [not before, not in place of] all we can do (2 Ne. 25:23).

First comes our reconciliation to the Lord wherein, by our very best efforts (works) we do all that we can to obey while manifesting (and admitting to both God and ourselves) our need for a power that is higher and stronger than our own. Then, when Christ judges that we have adequately paid the price by doing "all things that lie in our power," his grace will be applied, and the union of our works with his grace will bear fruit in the successful completion of our task.

The final words of Moroni also help clarify the joint

role of grace and works. As Moroni concluded his record, as he bid farewell to his readers and was ready to bury the plates, what was his final subject? The relationship between grace and works and Jesus Christ! Two of his last three verses in the Book of Mormon were dedicated to clarifying the part which each plays in achieving perfection! What a sobering thought this should be to those of us who have ignored or been embarrassed by references to grace.

> Yea, come unto Christ, and be perfected in him, and deny yourselves of all ungodliness; and if ye shall deny yourselves of all ungodliness and love God with all your might, mind and strength [works], then [after having done our part to the best of our ability] is his grace sufficient for you, that by his grace ye may be perfect in Christ; and if by the grace of God ye are perfect in Christ, ye can in nowise deny the power of God. [We will know that it was he which took us the rest of the way that we could not have gone on our own.]
>
> And again, [to be certain that we grasp the significance of this important doctrine] if ye by the grace of God are perfect in Christ, and deny not his power ["I made it by virtue of my own good works"], then are ye sanctified in Christ by the grace of God, through the shedding of the blood of Christ, which is in the covenant of the Father unto the remission of your sins, that ye become holy, without spot. (Moro. 10:32-33; see also 1 Cor. 15:9-10.)

President Kimball has given us these important words:

> Throughout the Church hundreds of thousands of faithful Saints have truly consecrated their lives and their energies to the work of the Lord, secure in the assurance that thereby they please him.
>
> It is a disappointment, however, to find many others who are not willing to trust the Lord—or to trust in his promise when he says, "Prove me and see." I often wonder why men cannot trust their Lord. He has promised his children every blessing contingent upon their faithfulness, *but*

> *fickle man places his trust in "the arm of flesh" and sets about to make his own way unaided by him who could do so much.* (1974-75 Melchizedek Priesthood Manual, *When Thou Art Converted, Strengthen Thy Brethren,* p. 86; emphasis added. See also Gal. 2:21; 2 Cor. 6:1.)

In the following parable former Church President, David O. McKay, makes clear the proper union of our best efforts with Christ's divine grace.

> One day, a group of small boys were swimming. Perhaps it would be more accurate to say they were learning to swim; for none could take more than a few strokes. Just below them a short distance down the stream was a treacherous hole much beyond their depth. Into this, either through bravado or accident, one daring youngster either plunged or fell. He became helpless to save himself; and for a moment his companions were powerless to aid him. Fortunately, one with presence of mind and quick action, jerked a long stick from a willow fence and held one end of it toward the drowning lad. The latter grasped it, held on tightly and was saved.
>
> All the boys declared that the venturesome lad owed his life to the boy who furnished the means of rescue.
>
> This is undoubtedly the fact; and yet in spite of the means furnished him, if the lad had not taken advantage of it, if he had not put forth all the personal effort at his command, he would have drowned, notwithstanding the heroic act of his comrade.
>
> In this old world of ours, children of men are playing, swimming, struggling in the sea of life. *There are those who claim that no one will sink and be lost if he will look to Jesus on the shore and say, "I believe." There are others who declare that every one must by his own efforts swim to the shore or be lost forever. The real truth is that both of these extremes are incorrect.* Christ redeemed all men from death which was brought upon them through no act of theirs, but he will not save men from their personal transgressions who will put forth no effort themselves, any more than the young rescuer on the river bank could have saved the drowning lad if the latter had not seized the means provided him. *Neither can man save himself without accepting the means provided by*

Christ for man's salvation. (The Gospel of Work, *Instructor,* January 1955, pp. 1-2; emphasis added.)

God Working In Us

Wherefore, my beloved, as ye have always obeyed, not as in my presence only, but now much more in my absence, work out your own salvation with fear and trembling.

For it is God which worketh in you both to will and to do of his good pleasure. (Philip. 2:12-13.)

And now, I do not know all things; but the Lord knoweth all things which are to come; wherefore, *he worketh in me to do according to his will* (W of M 7).

These two verses are among the most valuable we have to explain the miracle of Christ's grace working in us to "build us up" and compensate for our "gaps," as described earlier in the chapter. We notice in the second reference that the prophet, Mormon, living over three hundred years after Paul and, so far as we know, without a knowledge of Paul, gave almost the same words. What did Paul and Mormon mean by saying that God works inside us "both to will and to do," in order to accomplish in our lives the things which are according to "his good pleasure" or perfect will?

First, God working in us "to will:" We have all experienced the frustration of making promises to the Lord which we were not strong enough to keep. Jesus Christ working in us "to will" means that when we have made a righteous choice, and when our desire is to have our will in harmony with the Lord's will, but we lack the strength to see the commitment through to the end, the Savior will, upon our invitation, bestow his grace upon us. As his grace works within us, it will endorse and strengthen our will so that our preliminary gropings will be solidified into a firm and lasting resolve.

> Again, verily I say unto you, I will show unto you wisdom in me concerning all the churches, inasmuch as *they are willing to be guided in a right and proper way for their salvation*—
>
> That the work of the gathering together of my saints may continue, *that I may build them up* unto my name. . . (D&C 101:63-64.)

> . . . that we may present every man perfect in Christ Jesus:
>
> Whereunto I also labor, *striving according to his working, which worketh in me mightily.* (Col. 1:28-29.)

Second, God working in us "to do:" This means that having expanded and strengthened the will which we ourselves chose, the Lord then amplifies the power that is in us until it is "sufficient" to accomplish that chosen will. (His will and ours merged together.) In some marvelous way, his grace enables us to do what we had already chosen to do, but were too weak to accomplish on our own. Such is the marvelous promise to those who obediently seek to "work out their salvation with fear and trembling before him."

> Now the God of peace, that brought again from the dead our Lord Jesus, that great shepherd of the sheep, through the blood of the everlasting covenant,
>
> Make you perfect in every good work to do his will, *working in you that which is wellpleasing in his sight,* through Jesus Christ; (Heb. 13:20-21.)

> I can do all things through Christ which strengtheneth me (Philip. 4:13).

There are many, many scriptures which illustrate Christ's working in us both "to will and to do" as he builds us up and magnifies our efforts. The Savior said, for example, that if we would come to him with a humble acknowledgement of our need for his grace, he would cause our weaknesses to be converted to strengths.

> . . . for if they humble themselves before me, and have faith in me, then will I make weak things become strong unto them (Ether 12:27).

We struggle to be worthy before him, but Jesus taught that it is he who rewards the effort and gives the actual victory. "And inasmuch as ye are humble and faithful and call upon my name, behold, I will give you the victory" (D&C 104:82).

> And now, brethren, I commend you to God, and to the word of his grace, *which is able to build you up,* and to give you an inheritance among all them which are sanctified (Acts 20:32).

Growing In Grace

We have discussed the fact that we are to be expanded, purified, sanctified, and justified; that we are to conquer our sins and weaknesses, and ultimately achieve salvation and exaltation "through" the grace of Jesus Christ. But there is another concept of grace which we must also understand and apply. It is revealed in the following words:

> Wherefore, my beloved brethren, reconcile yourselves to the will of God, and not to the will of the devil and the flesh; and remember, after ye are reconciled unto God, that *it is only in and through the grace of God* that ye are saved (2 Ne. 10:24).

We learn from this verse that in addition to being saved "through" his grace, we must also be "in" a state of grace. What is the difference between being "in grace" and being saved "through grace"? It is learning to grow in grace. The Savior knows far better than we just how terribly far we each have to go before we can receive all that he has planned for us. Thus he has counseled and commanded that we, too, must "grow in grace."

> Behold, ye are little children and ye cannot bear all things now; *ye must grow in grace and in the knowledge of the truth* (D&C 50:40).

What would the Plan of Salvation be without eternal progression? How could we ever change from what we are now into what God has planned for us without the opportunity to climb step by step, line upon line, and precept upon precept? Growing "from grace to grace" was the path the Lord revealed to the Prophet Joseph Smith, who said:

> Here, then, is eternal life—to know the only wise and true God; and you have got to learn how to be Gods yourselves, and to be kings and priests to God, the same as all Gods have done before you, namely, *by going from one small degree to another, and from a small capacity to a great one; from grace to grace,* from exaltation to exaltation, until you attain to the resurrection of the dead, and are able to dwell in everlasting burnings, and to sit in glory, as do those who sit enthroned in everlasting power (*Teachings of the Prophet Joseph Smith,* 7th Ed., comp. Joseph Fielding Smith, S.L.C., Utah: Deseret Book Co., 1951, pp. 346-347; emphasis added).

In walking the paths of eternal progression we are following in the steps of our Savior. We should remember that even though he was sinless and pure throughout his life, he also had to grow from one level of grace to another. And thus it was that John said of him, "And he received not of the fulness at first, but *continued from grace to grace, until he received a fulness*" (D&C 93:13).

> Wherefore, redemption cometh *in* and *through* the Holy Messiah; for He is *full of grace* and truth (2 Ne. 2:6).

In following the example of our Savior, we, too, are expected to become "full of grace and truth." But we do not go from a state of partial grace into a state of full grace in one giant leap. Rather, we move from one level to the next through a life-long progression of experiences that bring Christ and his grace into our lives in an orderly growth process.

Grace is given more as an investment in our potential than as a reward, and God fully expects a return on his investment in us. (If we fully deserved the blessing, it would not be grace, but harvest.)

> There is another aspect of the law of the harvest, also of eternal significance. It is expressed in the familiar saying, "Where much is given, much is expected." (Luke 12:48.) When the Lord of the harvest has lavished great attention on a particular portion of his vineyard, he expects it to bear fruit, at least in proportion to the attention he has lavished. (President Dallin H. Oaks, Where Much Is Given, *Devotional Speeches of the Year,* Provo, Utah: Brigham Young University Press, 1978, p. 123.)

While we can never fully repay the Savior for his gifts to us, we can work toward that goal by being of service to others. "Freely ye have received, freely give" (Matt. 10:8). To better understand this principle, we may liken the flow of grace to the flow of water. Grace is not meant to simply flow into our lives as though its only purpose was to fill our own reservoir. Rather, it is meant to flow *through us* into the lives of others. Yes, it is true that when we first begin to enter the state of grace we are empty and, like a dry sponge, we are eager and thirsting to absorb all we can receive for our own needs. This is right and proper and, perhaps, at the beginning it is all we can do. The Savior himself said, "If any man thirst, let him come unto me, and drink" (John 7:37). But he also taught a most remarkable idea about our drinking from the waters of life. Not only are we to be filled with Christ's everlasting water, (never again thirsting ourselves, John 4:14.) but we are then meant to actually become like a well of water that flows into the lives of others who are also thirsting for relief from life's frustrations.

> But whosoever drinketh of the water that I shall give him shall never thirst; but the water that I shall give him shall be in him a well of water springing up into everlasting life (John 4:14).

This means that if we were only willing to absorb the flow of grace for ourselves, without giving out to the lives of those around us, our flow would soon stagnate and decay. Here, then, we discover an effect of grace that is most exciting. Once our own life is being healed through his grace, and once we are becoming spiritually alive and strong, the influence of the Savior's grace should spill over from us into the lives of others. And as we become partners with Christ and allow his grace to flow through us into the lives of those we serve, we find that our own capacity to receive expands. Thus it is that we follow the pattern set by the Savior as we learn to receive "grace for grace" (John 1:16).

> And I, John, saw that he [Jesus] received not of the fulness at the first, *but received grace for grace* (D&C 93:12).

> And may God grant, in his great fulness, that men might be brought unto repentance and good works, *that they might be restored unto grace for grace,* according to their works (Hel. 12:24).

> I give unto you these sayings that you may understand and know how to worship, and know what you worship, that you may come unto the Father in my name, and in due time receive of his fulness.
>
> For if you keep my commandments you shall receive of his fulness, and be glorified in me as I am in the Father; therefore, I say unto you, *you shall receive grace for grace.* (D&C 93:19-20.)

So we see that it is in giving service to others that we expand our own capacity and are then rewarded with "grace for grace." "Growing in grace" and receiving "grace for grace" is both our opportunity and our duty.

> As every man hath received the gift, even so minister the same one to another, as good stewards of the manifold grace of God (1 Pet. 4:10; see also Acts 20:35).
>
> Blessed by God, even the Father of our Lord Jesus Christ, the Father of mercies, and the God of all comfort;
> Who comforteth us in all our tribulation, *that we may be able to comfort them which are in any trouble, by the comfort wherewith we ourselves are comforted of God.* (2 Cor. 1:3-4.)
>
> Service is essential to salvation . . . We have to get outside of ourselves and do something for someone else, patterning our course after that of the Lord Jesus, if we are going to have an inheritance with him. (1979-80 Melchizedek Priesthood Manual, *He That Receiveth My Servants Receiveth Me,* p. 3.)

Falling From Grace

As a postscript we should add that the Lord has warned us through the Prophet Joseph Smith that after his grace has been bestowed, even after we have been justified and sanctified by it, even then, we may "fall from grace and depart from the living God!"

> And we know that justification through the grace of our Lord and Savior Jesus Christ is just and true;
> And we know also, that sanctification through the grace of our Lord and Savior Jesus Christ is just and true, to all those who love and serve God with all their mights, minds, and strength.
> But there is a possibility that man may fall from grace and depart from the living God;
> Therefore let the church take heed and pray always, lest they fall into temptation;

> Yea, and even let those who are sanctified take heed also. (D&C 20:30-34.)

When we receive the grace of the Savior to bless our lives, we come to know in a very special way that he is indeed a living and a caring God. This is a most precious and sacred gift. How careful we must be to respect and cherish it, even with "fear and trembling" as we "work out our salvation" before him. The blessings of grace draw us close to him in a wonderful bond of fellowship. To receive these blessings and then fail to honor them can cause us not only to "depart from the living God," but to develop a bitterness against our failure, alienating us from ourselves as well as the Savior.

> Follow peace with all men, and holiness, without which no man shall see the Lord:
>
> Looking diligently lest any man fail of the grace of God: lest any root of bitterness springing up trouble you, and thereby many be defiled. (Heb. 12:14-15.)

II
Does The Savior Understand?

Jesus Christ did not come to mortality as some kind of superhuman who was isolated or insulated from the problems which we experience. He suffered and was tempted just as we are—only more. If we are to exercise the faith in him which leads to salvation and exaltation, we must know that he understands our personal problems and that he truly cares about helping us to resolve them.

Was Jesus Really Mortal?

It is natural to have questions in our mind concerning the Savior's physical body. Was it really like ours? As the mortal offspring of God, how similar to our flesh was his flesh? How much of what we experience did he experience? How can we be certain that he really understands the weaknesses and temptations caused by our flesh and mortality? The answers to these questions are crucial to our belief that the Savior does understand our feelings and weaknesses by virtue of his own mortal experience.

One of the greatest barriers separating us from our Savior and weakening our faith in him is the false idea that he is so infinitely superior to us that he could never understand or empathize with our fears, hurts, weaknesses, discouragements, temptations, etc. It is true, of course, that

Christ is superior to us. Indeed, he is so infinitely superior that we cannot even begin to grasp the significance of his perfection. But his perfect holiness does not mean that he cannot understand us in our mortality. As Paul discussed Christ's role as our Savior, he stated that it was absolutely imperative that Jesus be made exactly like us "in all things" which he experienced except, of course, for sin.[3]

> Wherefore *in all things it behoved him to be made like unto his brethren,* that he might be a merciful and faithful high priest in things pertaining to God . . . (Heb. 2:17).
>
> But [He] made himself of no reputation, and took upon him the form of a servant, and was made in the likeness of men:
>
> *And being found in fashion as a man,* he humbled himself, and became obedient unto death, even the death of the cross. (Philip. 2:7-8.)

When Jesus agreed to come to the earth and minister as our Savior, he agreed to experience mortality in all its fullness. He came not as a spectator, but as a participant. It is true that he came as the Only Begotten of the Father in the flesh, and that this inheritance gave him power over physical death. (See John 10:17-18.) But, except for his sinlessness, his mortality was just as real as ours. Jesus was completely human. The scriptures present a major emphasis of the fact that the Savior took upon himself the experience of total mortality so that he would leave absolutely no barriers between his mortal experiences in the flesh and his understanding of our problems.

---

[3]Even though Christ lived in perfect sinlessness, he still understands the consequences of sin. His suffering in the Garden of Gethsemane was the result of his assuming the guilt, burdens, punishments, and effects of the total sin of each and all of mankind the same as if they had been committed by himself. This idea is discussed in more detail in chapter 16.

> For behold, the time cometh, and is not far distant, that with power, the Lord Omnipotent who reigneth, who was, and is from all eternity to all eternity, shall come down from heaven among the children of men, *and shall dwell in a tabernacle of clay*. . . (Mosiah 3:5.)

> Forasmuch then as the children are partakers of flesh and blood, he also himself likewise took part of the same. . . (Heb. 2:14.)

Could Jesus Christ have accomplished the atonement without enduring the indignities and sufferings inflicted upon him? Could he understand our problems if he had not struggled himself? The answer is no.

We are told by the Prophet Alma that Jesus could have chosen to view our sorrows, temptations, weaknesses and pains vicariously. He could have chosen to know them secondhand through the influence of the Holy Ghost which "knoweth all things." But, because of his infinite love, because he wanted no barriers to exist between him and us, because he wanted to be perfect in his atonement, and because he wanted to be perfect in his ability to empathize and to assist us in carrying our burdens, he chose to encounter the experiences of mortality firsthand, in the flesh, exactly as we do.

> And he shall go forth, *suffering pains and afflictions and temptations of every kind;* and this that the word might be fulfilled which saith he will take upon him the pains and the sicknesses of his people.
>
> . . . and he will take upon him their infirmities, that his bowels may be filled with mercy, *according to the flesh, that he may know according to the flesh how to succor his people according to their infirmities.*
>
> Now the Spirit knoweth all things; *nevertheless the Son of God suffereth according to the flesh* that he might take upon him the sins of his people, that he might blot out their transgressions according to the power of his deliverance. . . (Alma 7:11-13.)

The "power of his deliverance" is built upon the foundation of his personal, firsthand exposure, in his own flesh, to every kind of human pain, affliction, infirmity, and temptation possible. His exposure included physical afflictions as well as spiritual, mental, and emotional—"suffering pains and afflictions of *every* kind." Why did Jesus have to suffer? So that we can never suffer anything which is unfamiliar to his own experience.

> Even though He was God's Son sent to earth, the divine plan of the Father required that Jesus be subjected to all the difficulties and tribulations of mortality. . .
>
> Because He descended below all things (see D&C 122:8), He knows how to help us rise above our daily difficulties. . .
>
> Indeed there is no human condition—be it suffering, incapacity, inadequacy, mental deficiency, or sin—which He cannot comprehend or for which His love will not reach out to the individual. ("Jesus Christ: Our Savior and Redeemer," Ezra Taft Benson, *Ensign,* November 1983, pp. 6-8.)

His Descent Below All Things

If we were to contemplate, without a knowledge of the scriptures, in what manner a Divine Being might condescend to come among men to effect their salvation, we would never, never imagine that he would lower himself to our own level of experience. We would never dare to imagine that such a divine and perfectly holy being would or could descend to our level. But the truth is that Jesus did not merely descend to our level, he actually descended to a depth of experience far below our level. He experienced mortality to a degree far more total than our own.

> . . . know thou, my son, that all these things shall give thee experience, and shall be for thy good.
>
> The Son of Man hath descended below them all. Art thou greater than he? (D&C 122:7-8.)

> . . . he descended below all things, in that he comprehended all things, that he might be in all and through all things, the light of truth . . . (D&C 88:6).

In the last verse we are given the reason that Jesus "descended below all things." It was so that he would personally know and experience every human emotion, every temptation, every sorrow, every possible disappointment, every fear, every worry, etc. that we experience. And so that having thus experienced for himself, he could then minister to us "the light of truth" which we would need "in all and through all things" which we might experience. Jesus suffered to a level far below and beyond our experience so that we would never have reason to doubt that he really understands our feelings and our problems.

As the prophets looked forward in time and beheld the coming ministry of the Savior, they never ceased to marvel that he would come, not as a God, but first as a baby and then as a man like unto ourselves. Their greatest astonishment was always expressed over the suffering and indignities that Jesus would endure.

> Have they not said that God himself should come down among the children of men, and take upon him the form of man. . .
>
> Yea, and have they not said also . . . that he, himself, should be oppressed and afflicted? (Mosiah 13:34-35; see also Mark 9:12.)

> He is despised and rejected of men; a man of sorrows, and acquainted with grief . . . (Isa. 53:3; see also Mosiah 15:5).

I once had the privilege of guiding a man through his first reading of the New Testament. He knew almost nothing about the life and death of Christ. This reading was his first exposure to the cruelties inflicted upon the Savior. He was absolutely dumbfounded by the things which were done to him. "How is this possible?" he cried in astonishment. "They can't do that to Him!" But they did do it, and so we also ought to cry out in protest. But why did Jesus allow it when it would have been so easy to escape? It was because of his incomprehensible love for us.

> . . . wherefore they scourge him, and he suffereth it; and they smite him, and he suffereth it. Yea, they spit upon him, and he suffereth it, *because of his loving kindness* and his long-suffering towards the children of men. (1 Ne. 19:9.)

When the scriptures say that Jesus descended below all things, they mean that he suffered the pains of humanity in a totality that is beyond our comprehension. There were two parts of this totality: the first part was the severity of his suffering, and the second part was the inclusion of every possible facet of humanity's burdens.

Jesus suffered to an intensity that would have instantly crushed the life from our bodies. Only his power over death enabled him to endure the crushing pain without dying. His anguish on our behalf was so great that it caused his precious blood to ooze from every pore!

> And lo, he shall suffer temptations, and pain of body, hunger, thirst, and fatigue, even more than man can suffer, except it be unto death; for behold, blood cometh from every pore, so great shall be his anguish for the wickedness and the abominations of his people (Mosiah 3:7).

Why was his pain so great? Because it was all inclusive. He felt the "wickedness and abominations" of every mortal that has lived or that will yet live upon this planet. Most of us have had pain and disappointment in our life. Though we may not have known it then, we can now know that Jesus was already a part of that pain. In the Garden of Gethsemane, and perhaps again on the cross, as the Savior looked backward and forward through the corridors of time, he somehow envisioned the total sorrow of every human that ever had or ever would live upon the earth and took that pain upon himself. As Isaiah said, "In *all* their affliction he was afflicted" (Isa. 63:9). As astounding and incomprehensible as this is to our finite minds, Jesus Christ has already been, and will continue to be, a part of every tear that we shed.

> . . . wherefore he suffered the pain of all men, that all men might repent and come unto him (D&C 18:11; see also Ps 69:20).
>
> And he cometh into the world that he may save all men if they will hearken unto his voice; for behold, he suffereth the pains of all men, yea, the pains of every living creature, both men, women, and children, who belong to the family of Adam (2 Ne. 9:21; see also Lam. 1:12).
>
> It was in Gethsemane where Jesus took on Himself the sins of the world, in Gethsemane where *His pain was equivalent to the cumulative burden of all men,* in Gethsemane where He descended below all things so that all could repent and come to Him.
>
> The mortal mind fails to fathom, the tongue cannot express, the pen of man cannot describe the breadth, depth, or height of the suffering of our Lord—or His infinite love for us. (Ezra Taft Benson, The Marks of the Divinity of Jesus Christ, *Ensign,* December 1980, p. 47; emphasis added.)

What a comfort it is to know that no sorrow we will ever experience is beyond the comprehension and compassion of Christ's tender affection. No matter how long we have felt estranged from him, no matter what our reasons were for avoiding him, when we return to him, we will always discover that he was there all the time, waiting patiently and hopefully, yearning for an invitation to join in our battle.

> Surely he hath borne our griefs, and carried our sorrows . . . (Isa. 53:4.)

Were His Temptations Real?

It was not only in the depth and breadth of his suffering that Christ descended below the level of our experiences, but also in his temptations. How vital it is that we understand this truth.

Immediately following his baptism by John, Jesus went into the wilderness to be alone with God as he made final preparations for his ministry. It is common knowledge that Jesus was tempted three times by Satan during those forty days in the wilderness. (See Matt. 4:1-11.) It is sometimes assumed that those three encounters were the end of his temptations, but this is not true. Such a brief encounter with temptation could never have given Christ the great compassion that he manifests for our weaknesses and sins; a compassion that proves his comprehension of the battles of "real life."

The scripture records that at the end of those wilderness temptations the devil only "departed from Him for a season" (Luke 4:13). We know that the Savior's temptations continued throughout the entire three years of his ministry because it was at the Last Supper that he said to his Twelve Apostles, "Ye are they which have continued with me in my temptations" (Luke 22:28). Since none of them were with him in the wilderness temptations, this statement can only refer to the temptations which occurred during his three-year ministry. Far more important, however, than the length of time Jesus was tempted, is the fact that he personally had to confront and overcome every possible temptation known to man.

> For we have not an high priest which cannot be touched (Greek translation: unable to sympathize with our frailties and imperfections) with the feeling of our infirmities; *but was in all points tempted like as we are, yet without sin.*
>
> Let us therefore come boldly unto the throne of grace, that we may obtain mercy, and find grace to help in time of need. (Heb. 4:15-16.)

Think about the wonderful implications of that remarkable statement. Paul is presenting the reality of Christ's temptations as the very reason we can have confidence, and even boldness, in approaching God for mercy, help, and grace.

Was Jesus so holy that it was easy for him to resist these temptations? Was his exposure to temptation "in all points" merely an academic overview, or was it a real encounter like (or even worse than) ours? The answer from the scriptures is that the resistance to his constant temptations was a major part of his "sufferings." Many of the scriptural references to the Savior's temptations include the word, "suffer," in their descriptions. Consider three examples:

> And he shall go forth, *suffering* pains and afflictions and *temptations of every kind*. . . (Alma 7:11).

> He *suffered temptations* but gave no heed unto them (D&C 20:22).

> (And He) suffereth temptation, and yieldeth not to the temptation. . . (Mosiah 15:5).

How would it be possible for the Son of God to *"suffer"* in his resistance to temptation unless they were real and genuine encounters? How could he suffer unless he was truly tempted? We cannot comprehend the intensity and determination with which Satan would have marshalled his evil forces against the Lord, but we can be certain that he urgently tried to destroy Jesus Christ more than any other person who has ever lived. Perhaps we can glimpse the terrible struggle Christ endured because of his temptations when we read Paul's statement concerning him as our High Priest, "who in the days of his flesh . . . offered up prayers and supplications with strong crying and tears. . ." (Heb. 5:7).

It was not by avoiding and escaping the realities of life's sins that the Savior's holiness was perfected. No man ever walked the earth more conscious of sin than Jesus Christ. His holiness and purity came, as should ours, by the resistance and conquest of sin. The more we resist, the holier we are. (See James 1:12.) The greater our victory, the more Christlike we will be. No wonder the Savior is so hesitant to condemn. No wonder he is so anxious to forgive. He knows better than any other the price required for victory over temptation. Let us remember that if Jesus, who was totally innocent of sin, was actually tempted to the point of suffering, then it is no sin for us to be tempted—it is a part of mortality.

> For in that he himself hath suffered being tempted, he is able to succour them that are tempted (Heb. 2:18).
>
> . . . the Lord your God, even Jesus Christ, your advocate, who knoweth the weakness of man and how to succor them who are tempted (D&C 62:1).

He Came To Care

When Jesus returned to Nazareth, where he was rejected by the offended people of his own home town, he had already been baptized by John, tempted in the wilderness, and begun his ministry and the selection of his closest disciples. By then his fame had created great curiosity among his former neighbors. As he entered the synagogue, they gave him the place of honor to read from the scriptures. Jesus knew that this occasion would become a pivotal point, not only for the people of Nazareth's understanding and faith, but also for the countless millions who would someday read the words which he chose for this description of his ministry. There would be no other moment in all his life to parallel this occasion. What one simple scripture could he choose to best symbolize or describe the purpose and duty of his calling? He chose a verse from Isaiah:

> The Spirit of the Lord is upon me, because he hath annointed me to preach the gospel to the poor; he hath sent me to heal the brokenhearted, to preach deliverance to the captives, and recovering of sight to the blind, to set at liberty them that are bruised . . . . (Luke 4:18; compare Isa. 61:1).

Isn't it interesting, and significant to our study, that of all the hundreds of prophecies of his ministry which he could have chosen to signify his role as the promised Messiah, he chose this one? It did not speak of kingdoms or programs. He chose instead, a verse which speaks of his tender mercy and compassion upon those who sorrow with mental bruises and broken hearts; of those who are held captive by the enslavement of bitterness and sin. There was no pronouncement of power or glory, no threat to the Roman conquerors, no criticism of the misguided rabbis or priests. Just a beautiful emphasis of his desire to be a part of our personal life by showing love, compassion and understanding for our broken hearts, for our mental and emotional hurts and bruises. He said that he came to give the power and the truth to restore our spiritual vision and to release us from the captivity of enslaving habits. He came with the mission to release us, through the power of his love and forgiveness, into a life full of abundance and joy. (See John 10:10; 2 Ne. 2:25.) His greatest desire is not for personal fame or position, but to wrap us in the arms of his love (D&C 6:20) and remove from us all that holds us back from being what we were meant to be. How great was, and is, his desire to convince each one of us that we are important and precious to him.

> Come unto me, all ye that labour and are heavy laden, and I will give you rest.
>
> Take my yoke upon you, and learn of me; for I am meek and lowly in heart: and ye shall find rest unto your souls.
>
> For my yoke is easy, and my burden is light. (Matt. 11:28-30.)

The Savior is still trying to become our friend, to become involved in our lives to such a degree that he can assume for us the actual pains, sicknesses, infirmities and burdens which weigh so heavily upon us. He is the source of the peace and rest for which we hunger. We do not have to understand the miracle of this transition in order to experience its relief. He has invited every person to "come" to him. Many can testify that they have accepted his kind invitation and have come away both happier and holier.

III
The "Devices" Of Satan

As the God of this world, Satan uses every imaginable device to deceive us, to discourage, entice and enslave us, and to distract us from the power of Christ's redemption. His power to do so is awesome, as is his anger and determination. I never comprehended the intensity of his hate toward us until I was excommunicated, and came face to face with the unwavering determination of Satan and his evil followers to enslave and destroy our souls.

Satan Desireth To Have You

In his relentless endeavor to capture our souls, Satan travels across the entire face of the earth training, counseling, and motivating the wicked army of evil spirits who have joined themselves to his cause. Planning the treacherous strategies to be used against us, he exerts his evil leadership unceasingly among his hosts who are stationed throughout every inhabited part of the earth.

> And thus he goeth up and down, to and fro in the earth, seeking to destroy the souls of men (D&C 10:27; see also Job 1:7).

> Be sober, be vigilant; because your adversary the devil, as a roaring lion, walketh about, seeking whom he may

> devour (1 Peter 5:8; see also Rev. 12:12).
>
> . . . for the devil is an enemy unto God, and fighteth against him continually, and inviteth and enticeth to sin, and to do that which is evil continually (Moro. 7:12).

Lucifer has vast multitudes of evil followers to assist him in the war for our souls. It is important to consider some numbers. It has been estimated that the population of the spirit world is approximately seventy billion people who have previously lived upon the earth. (Neal Maxwell, *Notwithstanding My Weaknesses,* S.L.C., Utah: Deseret Book Co., 1981, p. 55.) Seventy billion spirits there plus five billion mortals alive today equals seventy-five billion people. If we were to assume that this number represents the two-thirds of God's children who were to be privileged to come to earth in mortal bodies (not counting those who are yet to come), then we could calculate that the hosts of Satan (the remaining third of God's spirit children) who rebelled and were cast down to war against us would number over thirty-seven billion!

This staggering number would mean that Satan has at his command at least seven evil spirits against each mortal alive on the earth today. But the odds are even greater than that, for he does not divide his spirits against us equally. The prophets have told us that Satan concentrates his forces against the righteous. Therefore, we could easily conclude that every person who is sincerely striving for a righteous life could be surrounded and tempted by thirty, forty, perhaps even hundreds of evil spirits. Whatever the exact numbers are, we know that we are literally surrounded by the hosts of Satan, and that his forces vastly outnumber us. (See D&C 29:36; Rev. 12:4, 9; Abr. 3:27-28.) The importance of living worthy of the companionship, protection, and inspiration of the Holy Ghost is obvious.

> Behold, we are surrounded by demons, yea, we are encircled about by the angels of him who hath sought to destroy our souls (Hel. 13:37; see also D&C 50:2).

> Wherefore, he maketh war with the saints of God, and encompasseth them round about (D&C 76:29).

There is no shame felt by Satan or his angels. Their war against God and righteousness is one of arrogant defiance. In his miserable existence, Satan's only reward—his only pleasure—is the victory he achieves over the souls of men. The scriptures teach that he not only laughs and takes delight in our destruction, but that as he revels in his conquest, he contemptuously laughs at the heavens. Truly, Satan desires to possess each one of us.

> . . . and Enoch was high and lifted up, even in the bosom of the Father, and of the Son of Man; and behold, the power of Satan was upon all the face of the earth.
>
> And he beheld Satan; and he had a great chain in his hand, and it veiled the whole face of the earth with darkness; *and he looked up and laughed, and his angels rejoiced.* (Moses 7:24, 26.)

Satan is not the arch enemy of God because he threatens God's divine power, but because of his threat to us, the children of God. One of his greatest threats is the distortion and ridicule of the truth. Lest we become free from him by comprehending and obeying truth, every time we try to improve our knowledge of the gospel, Satan's followers are there to rush into our learning experience and do all within their power to discredit the truth, or to remove it from our minds and hearts. (See Matt. 13:19; Mark 4:14-15; Luke 8:11-12.)

> . . . Satan seeketh to turn their hearts away from the truth, that they become blinded and understand not the things which are prepared for them (D&C 78:10; see also 3 Ne. 1:19-22; 2:2-3).

> Behold, verily I say unto you, that there are many spirits which are false spirits, which have gone forth in the earth, deceiving the world.
>
> And also Satan hath sought to deceive you, that he might overthrow you. (D&C 50:2-3; see also Matt. 13:19; Mark 4:14-19; Luke 8:11-12.)

Because of this negative and confusing influence, we need the spiritual discernment which comes from prayer and the Holy Ghost to know what is true, and just how we should apply it in our lives. If we are to be strengthened and expanded by the Savior's grace, if we are to survive the spiritual war between Christ and Lucifer, then we must understand and guard ourselves against Satan's devices. However, we need not live in *fear* of Satan's army as long as we honor our sacrament covenants and live in tune with the Holy Ghost.[4]

He Whispereth In Their Ears

Why is it so terribly hard to break free of the faults, weaknesses and sins which hold us in bondage? You already know part of the reason: it is simply because we are creatures of habit. You also know that habits can be changed—if we really want to change them. But there is another reason why change and improvement are so difficult. No matter how sincere we are, something seems to hold us back, for Satan is committed to keep us at the point of our defeat. He hates us and is determined to thwart our every effort to change and grow. How does he do this? He does it by "whispering" lies in our ears which discourage and confuse us. If we are ever to break free from our bonds and find the peace and victory

---

[4]While this chapter was originally intended as an appendix, it has been placed here at the beginning of the book to forewarn the reader of Satan's intent to oppose his efforts to move closer to the Lord.

we yearn for, it is vital that we understand Satan's ability to tempt and deceive us by direct, personal, and individual communication between our spirit and the evil spirits which follow him. Nephi said that Satan (and, of course, his followers) can actually speak to us without our being consciously aware of it. They do this by "whispering" in our ears.

> And others will he pacify, and lull them away into carnal security, that they will say: All is well in Zion; yea, Zion prospereth, all is well—and thus the devil cheateth their souls, and leadeth them away carefully down to hell.
>
> And behold, others he flattereth away, and telleth them there is no hell; and he saith unto them: I am no devil, for there is none—*and thus he whispereth in their ears,* until he grasps them with his awful chains, from whence there is no deliverance. (2 Ne. 28:21-22.)

"Whispering" in our spiritual ears means that Satan's evil spirits have the power to suggest thoughts and feelings directly to our spirit even though we are unaware of it happening with our mortal, conscious mind. His "whisperings" cause the suggested thoughts and feelings to be transmitted through our spirit to our conscious mind as if we had thought of them ourselves. Consider the following account of two missionaries in Samoa, Elders Edward Wood and Brigham Smoot. Their experience illustrates how a spirit can speak to a mortal man and cause thoughts to occur in the conscious mind, even though the individual is not consciously aware of the communication or the source of the idea.

> Probably the most remarkable experience of Elder Wood's first mission resulted from a missionary's disobedience to his mother's counsel. When Brigham Smoot left for his mission to Samoa, he promised his mother that he would not go swimming out in the sea. Only one day after his arrival in Samoa, he was persuaded by Edward to join the

> group for the usual bath at sea. As the new elder was wading out to sea, he slipped and fell into a deep hole in the reef. As he was unable to swim, he soon dropped to the bottom of the hole.
>
> Edward had promised to be responsible for the new elder's safety, and noticing him absent, he began a frantic search. Brigham Smoot was soon found in the attitude of prayer at the bottom of the hole. His limp body was dragged from the hole and carried to the beach. Blood was flowing from his eyes, nose and mouth. Elder Wood said of his companion, "He was perfectly lifeless and dead." In vain the elders used all normal restorative measures. By this time a large crowd of inquisitive natives had gathered around. Their telling of a native boy who had previously drowned in the same hole brought no comfort to the worried missionaries.
>
> *Elder Wood said that at this time he felt inspired by the spirit* that the only way his companion's spirit could re-enter his body would be to administer to him. Accordingly the body of Elder Smoot was dressed in clean garments and a new suit of clothes. The superstitious natives warned against such treatment of the body, and thought it sacrilegious to tamper with life and death. *Obedient to the inspiration,* however, the body was annointed. While Elder Wood was sealing the annointing, he felt life come back to Elder Smoot's body. Shortly after the administration, Elder Smoot talked with the missionaries and bore solemn testimony to them. He told of how, in the spirit, he watched them recover his body from the hole, take it to the beach and try to restore it to life. *He also told of touching Elder Wood on the shoulder and telling him that the only way to bring life back into the body was to use the priesthood which he bore.* (Duane S. Crowther, *Life Everlasting,* S.L.C., Utah: Bookcraft, Inc., pp. 47-48, original sources cited therein; emphasis added.)

We notice that when the drowned elder's spirit touched the shoulder of his companion and spoke into his ear, instructing him to use the priesthood, that same thought occurred in his companion's conscious mind, who then felt impressed or inspired to do so. Undoubtedly every reader has experienced the sudden appearance of evil thoughts which had no possible origin in his previous train of thought.

Many such thoughts and feelings may be prompted by Satan's whisperings. I have learned that one of Satan's favorite devices is to first suggest a wicked or negative thought, and then whisper to us the idea that the presence of such thoughts within us is proof of our inferiority and unworthiness.[5]

Because we are surrounded by Satan's treacherous demons who constantly whisper evil and discouraging suggestions to us, we must learn not to automatically respond to such thoughts with feelings of self-condemnation. All people experience unworthy and discouraging thoughts. The important factor in judging our righteousness is not the appearance of an unworthy thought, but our response once the thought has appeared. Do we enjoy the thought and allow it to develop? Do we contemplate and wish for its fulfillment? Or do we reject it and turn our attention to more holy considerations?

Many General Authorities have reported experiences with Satan's "whisperings" similar to the following report by Heber J. Grant in general conference in April 1941.

> There are two spirits striving with us always, one telling us to continue our labor for good [the Holy Ghost], and one telling us that with the faults and failing of our nature we are unworthy. I can truthfully say that from October 1882 until February 1883, that spirit followed me day and night telling me that I was unworthy to be an Apostle of the Church and I ought to resign.
>
> When I would testify of my knowledge that Jesus is the Christ, the Son of the Living God, the Redeemer of mankind, *it seemed as though a voice would say to me:* "You lie! You

---

[5]Satan's power to plant thoughts and feelings in our mind through his whisperings does not mean that he can read our own thoughts which are already there in our mind. (See D&C 6:16.)

> lie! You have never seen him."[6] (Quoted in *Faith Precedes The Miracle,* Spencer W. Kimball, S.L.C., Utah: Deseret Book Co., 1972, pp. 37-39; emphasis added. See also JS-H 20; Zech. 3:1.)

John reports that it was not Judas, himself, that conceived the idea of betraying the Lord, but that he chose to accept the idea of betrayal which Satan planted in his mind. (See John 13:2.) In similar testimony, Peter witnessed to the Church that it was also Satan who "filled the hearts" of Ananias and Sapphira to try and deceive him regarding their financial contributions. (See Acts 5:1-3.)[7]

Not all of Satan's whisperings are plainly evil. Often he will attempt to distract and confuse by prompting us to substitute a lesser good for a greater good. Consider the scheming distortion of truth which he whispered to Tohru Hotta, a Japanese convert, as was later related in a letter to the missionary who taught him the gospel.

> When I joined the Church, I didn't fully understand the deep significance of the law of tithing. However, I knew and trusted you, Elder Dan Hawkley, and I made a promise to you to pay tithing. I could tell you were anxious that I should keep that promise.
>
> I could not forget the challenge I had been given. However, to be honest, I must admit that I was anxious to buy a beautiful and glittering Japanese Bible like the one you had. I wanted it to help me remember what I had been taught, as well as to remember the elder who had helped to teach me. But it was too expensive for me to buy one.
>
> I reasoned that if I didn't pay my tithing, I could obtain the Bible. *Satan spoke in a whisper:* "Buy it. It's your money.

---

[6]President Grant then related a vision in which it was made known to him that he was worthy and had been divinely called.

[7]For an account of similar deceptions by Satan, see D&C 10:15, 20; 63:28; Alma 12:4-5; Hel. 6:26-30.

> Don't worry."
>
> But, dear elder, I couldn't forget your challenge. I knew it had come through the power of the holy priesthood and the Holy Spirit. I didn't buy that Bible. I paid my tithing instead. And because I overcame that challenge, I came to really understand the meaning of tithing as a covenant between the Lord and myself. (*The New Era,* December 1979, p. 13; emphasis added.)

While the ability of Satan's hosts to surround us and whisper lies to us is alarming, we should rejoice in the knowledge that through the influence of the Holy Ghost we can discern and reject all of their encroachments. Satan can have absolutely no power over our mind and heart except as we allow.

> And because of the righteousness of his people, Satan has no power . . . for he hath no power over the hearts of the people, for they dwell in righteousness, and the Holy One of Israel reigneth. (1 Ne. 22:26.)

The Father Of All Lies

Satan's strategy of conquest is built upon deception and distortion. Yet, when we hear his whisperings, we are quick to forget how skilled he is at making his lies sound reasonable.

> The Savior said that the very elect would be deceived by Lucifer if it were possible. He will use his logic to confuse and his rationalizations to destroy. He will shade meanings, open doors an inch at a time, and lead from purest white through all the shades of gray to the darkest black.
>
> Young people are confused by the arch deceiver, who uses every device to deceive them. (Spencer W. Kimball, *Faith Precedes the Miracle,* 3rd Ed., S.L.C., Utah: Deseret Book Co., 1973, pp. 152-153; see also Moses 4:4 John 8:44; Ether 8:25; D&C 50:3; 52:14.)

We have learned that Satan and his billions of evil spirits surround us continually. They whisper to us; they shout; they taunt; they lie; they do all within their power to deceive, discourage, and distract us. Let us now briefly review some of the most common lies which Satan uses for our destruction.

Lie Number 1: "It Mattereth Not"

One of Satan's most persistent goals is the contradiction of our conscience. Thus he whispers that "all is well" (2 Ne. 28:21); there is no devil or hell or standard of evil (2 Ne. 28:22); things aren't so bad just because we sin—after all, no one is perfect; and, trying to nullify our conscience, he whispers that we should not be so hard on ourselves, that we should "give in and be our real self."

These treacherous whisperings represent one of Lucifer's most blatant lies, which is the liberalism of man's right to do as he pleases without facing consequences. Over and over he and his followers whisper that we may do as we please, for "there is no harm in this," and "it mattereth not." (See Morm. 8:31; 2 Ne. 28:8.)

Lie Number 2: "It Is Our Duty To Condemn Ourselves"

The purpose of this lie is to have us believe that simply because we have faults we are rejected by God, and that the only hope of ever pleasing him is to condemn ourselves. This lie is contradictory to the first, but it is effective against many who are not deceived by the "it mattereth not" philosophy.

Many people who are living lives of misery and shame, who feel far from God, and who feel unworthy of his love would be surprised, and even resentful, of the suggestion that their unhappiness is a form of sin. Yet, without realizing that the lie came from Satan, they believe it is their duty to feel miserable because of their unworthiness. It is a well-known law of mental function that whatever holds your attention holds you. Thus, having been deceived by Satan, they continue on and on in their self-imposed prison, locking out of their hearts the healing influence of a Savior who longs to lift them above their sins to freedom, victory and joy.

Lie Number 3: "It Is Our Duty To Hold Grudges Against Ourselves"

Because we make mistakes, Satan would have us believe it is our duty to resent our fallibility by bearing grudges against ourselves. A grudge has been defined as "a cherished feeling of resentment or ill will that seeks satisfaction." When Satan can inspire such self-hatred, he has set us up for lie number 4.

> Grudge not one against another [or yourself], brethren, lest ye be condemned. . . (James 5:9).

Lie Number 4: "It Is Our Duty To Punish Ourselves For Our Sins"

Satan uses this lie to make us believe that we can please God by punishing ourselves. *"See, look at me, God. See how angry I am with myself over my weaknesses and sins? See how miserable I can make myself to please you?"* What an awful distortion.

No one has the right to take such power into his own hands. Judgment and punishment belong to God. He alone has the ability to judge fairly and to prescribe the appropriate punishment. We cannot hasten our salvation by self-punishment! How many times do we suffer the loss of forgiveness, not because it was withheld by the Lord, but simply because it is blocked by the overwhelming presence of our own self-punishment.

Lie Number 5: "It Is Our Duty To Feel Bitterness Toward Ourselves"

Since the process of self-condemnation and self-punishment (lies number 2, 3, 4) is so uncomfortable, Satan whispers that it is only right and normal to feel bitterness toward ourselves. In fact, it is our duty. After all, just look how miserable we have made ourselves.

When we indulge grudges and feelings of vengeance, bitterness, wrath, and malice toward ourselves, we tend to perpetuate our faults by blocking out their cure. Such feelings are the emotional equivalent of poison. And, by indulging them, we open the door to Satan's helpers who are thrilled to rush in and prompt us to over-emphasize these feelings of inferiority, unworthiness and resentment.

> Let all bitterness, and wrath, and anger . . . be put away from you, with all malice (Eph. 4:31; see also 2 Ne. 26:32).

Lie Number 6: "The More Guilty We Feel, The More Repentant We Are"

It is certainly proper to have guilty feelings about our faults—to a point. (See Num. 32:23; Ezek. 20:43; Alma 42:29; 2 Cor. 7:9-10.) Seizing upon our sincerity, however, Satan would have us expand and amplify our guilt and shame until he twists our proper emotions into an evil result. (See Ps. 40:12; Ezra 9:5-6.) Sometimes Satan persuades us to cling to our guilt as a substitute for repentance. Many well-meaning saints have been tricked into punishing themselves for their faults by clinging to their feelings of guilt and unworthiness. In some distorted way, Satan convinces us with this lie that the more guilty we feel, the more holy we are. This is a grievous error, for instead of drawing us closer to the Lord through repentance, over-emphasized guilt pulls us away from him through self-depreciation.

The proper response to feelings of shame and unworthiness is to repent and to do all that we can to put our lives in order. Then we must place the rest in the hands and grace of Jesus Christ, who has promised to show mercy as he removes the guilt from our repentant hearts. (See D&C 38:14; Enos 1:5-8; Alma 24:10.)

Satan has used the last 6000 years to develop thousands of clever deceptions, the analysis of which could justify an entire book. Do any of the following sound familiar?

"It will hurt too much to deal with this now. You will be far more comfortable if you put if off for awhile."

"There is no use praying about this until you have repented."

"God won't listen to you now, not after what you have done."

"Since you have already gone this far, you might as well go ahead and ___________."

"Since you've already done ___________, you may as well go ahead and enjoy it awhile before you start your repentance."

"You are unhappy because you married the wrong person. If you will find a new partner, you will be happier."

"There is no point in discussing this with your bishop. He will only look down on you. Or, he would not understand anyway."

"Surely God lied when he said he forgives and forgets. No one could ever forget this sin, especially not God, who 'knows all things.'"

With these lies and countless others, Satan works his devices to attract our attention away from the truth, power and redemption which centers in Jesus Christ. He and his followers do all they can to belittle us in our own eyes, to make us feel unworthy and unimportant. They do all they can to draw us away from the Savior and to destroy our faith and hope. How fervently we must pray that our eyes will be opened and that we will have the power to discern and reject their encroachments.

IV
Weaknesses

The Four Sources Of Our Weaknesses

As we seek to increase our spirituality and to deepen our relationship with God, there is probably nothing so restrictive to our efforts as the awareness of our weaknesses and faults. A feeling of regret for our weaknesses is common to all who become spiritually sensitized and who make it their major purpose in life to draw closer to God. In fact, the more earnestly we strive to approach God, the more sensitive we become to our weaknesses and failings. Such feelings are both natural and good because they direct us toward the appropriate actions required to become more Christlike.

But these feelings may also be dangerous if we are not careful. Why? Because Satan, knowing how we feel, rushes into our thoughts with the very believable lie that our weaknesses prove that we are neither worthy nor capable of achieving the spiritual goals we are seeking. Believing his lying deceptions can destroy our confidence and cause our weaknesses to form barriers between us and God.

Therefore, it is important that we differentiate between our weaknesses and our sins. In the 1977-78 Melchizedek Priesthood Manual we are taught that weaknesses and limitations are not necessarily sins.

> *Not all our weaknesses or limitations are sin.* Yet these weaknesses may still impede our own and other's progress or they may become stepping-stones for mighty achievement (*What Manner of Men Ought Ye To Be?* p. 139; emphasis added).

Of course some weaknesses are sinful. When we can identify that a weakness was self-imposed, that is to say, that its cause lies in the accumulation of our deliberate and improper choices, then we have identified a need for repentance, as with any sin. Such a condition is one for which we are fully responsible, and which represents a negative trait in our character. This is a condition for which it is proper to feel guilt and remorse. It is a weakness which we should desire to overcome so that we might become more worthy before the Lord. Yet, some of our weaknesses and limitations neither originate nor result in sin.

One of the most important keys to establishing a proper attitude about our weaknesses then, is to understand their origin. The 1977-78 Melchizedek Priesthood Manual identifies several possible origins of our weaknesses.

> There are many kinds of weaknesses—physical and spiritual. Some are general and come as a result of the limitations and bounds of mortality to which we are all subject; some are unique and are either permitted or given by a benevolent Father in Heaven. Other weaknesses are acquired by man through training, neglect, or by accident. Regardless of the source of the weakness, our response should be to strive either to overcome it or transform it into a strength. *Our sin is not that we are weak, but rather that we do not strive to rise above our weaknesses.* (*What Manner Of Men Ought Ye To Be?*, p. 139; emphasis added.)

It is vital to our spiritual progress that we grasp the difference and the responsibility for each of these different origins of weaknesses. The four main sources are as follows:

1. Those that are "permitted or given" to us—that is,

planted within our individual personality and genetic characteristics by a loving God for his divine purposes.

2. Those that all people have as a normal result of being in the state of mortality.

3. Those that we acquire as a consequence of the training (or neglect) we received from our parents and environment during the formative years.

4. Those that we create within ourselves as a consequence of our own sinful choices.

It is natural for a person who fails to understand these four sources of weaknesses to assume that all his personal weaknesses are of his own making, but this is never true. When we falsely assume responsibility for *all* our weaknesses, the next idea that follows is that they present an indisputable evidence of our unworthiness before God. If this evil deception from Satan is accepted, it will undermine our strongest efforts to reach God, for we will not have confidence nor will we believe that we can become close to him until *after* we have conquered our weaknesses. To believe that we are totally responsible for every weakness does a terrible injustice to our feelings of self-worth, and it is a complete contradiction to the revealed truth, for it was Jesus Christ, himself, who said in simple and unmistakable language, "I give unto men weaknesses . . ." (Ether 12:27).

This revelation surprises many who feel that it somehow contradicts what we know about the perfect and holy nature of God. But the truth is that the bestowal of divinely selected weaknesses is one of the greatest evidences we have of God's personal love and plan for each individual. Our Heavenly Father and Savior have gone to a great deal of trouble to select and implant within our beings the individual and specific weaknesses and characteristics which will be of most value in the process of seeking our exaltation and perfection.

Every sales manager would be pleased to have only "super-salesmen" on his team, but if he is to make a success of his business, he must begin with the men or women just as they are, and not as he wishes them to be. So it is with the successful coach, or teacher, or with anyone who works with people. And so it is with God. His gospel is not designed for the few whose mighty spiritual powers tower above the masses of humanity. His plan of salvation is designed to accommodate all who will come to him. It is "adapted to the capacity of the weak and the weakest of all saints. . ." (D&C 89:3). And so it was that he brought forth the gospel, not for the already strong and mighty, but to "prepare the weak for those things which are coming on the earth. . ." (D&C 133:58).

> For ye see your calling, brethren, how that not many wise men after the flesh, not many mighty, not many noble, are called:
>
> But . . . God hath chosen the weak things of the world to confound the things which are mighty. (1 Cor. 1:26-27.)

Perhaps we can now realize why there is such a vast difference between the way we see our weaknesses and the way God views them. In our distorted pride, we almost always look upon them in shame, not realizing that God never rejects anyone simply because they have unconquered weaknesses. I believe what matters most to him is not that we have weaknesses, but what we are doing about them. If a weakness is not related to the consequences of our own sinful choices, then its origin must lie within the other three sources which God has either "given or permitted" to occur within our creation and formative environment.

The weaknesses, then, which come from one of the first three sources identified in the 1977-78 Priesthood Manual (and which are listed on pages 46 & 47 of this chapter) do not represent negative forces in our life, but positive ones. They are not obstacles, but opportunities. It would be both ignorant and ungrateful on our part to feel resentment toward God (or ourselves) for the very conditions of life and character which present us with opportunities for growth and strength.

> Nay but, O man, who art thou that repliest against God? Shall the thing formed say to him that formed it, Why hast thou made me thus?
>
> Hath not the potter power over the clay, of the same lump to make one vessel unto honour, and another unto dishonour? (Rom. 9:20-21.)
>
> But by the grace of God I am what I am. . . (1 Cor. 15:10).

If God does not reject or condemn us for having unconquered weaknesses, then what right do we have to judge and condemn ourselves or others? Of course, we want to improve ourselves, but inasmuch as he is allowing us both time and room to grow, we must be humble enough to stop condemning ourselves and take advantage of it. Let us heed Nephi's counsel:

> . . . not that I would excuse myself because of other men, but because of the weakness which is in me, according to the flesh, I would excuse [or refrain from condemning] myself (1 Ne. 19:6).

On the other hand, we are not suggesting that one should accept Satan's "it mattereth not" lies and simply dismiss all his weaknesses with a shrug of the shoulders. To do so would be spiritual suicide.

> "Sorry, but that is the way I am . . . I was like this in the beginning, am now, and ever shall be . . ." is a handy motto and delusion to have around if you don't want to grow up. (John Powell, S.J., *Why Am I Afraid To Tell You Who I Am?*, Chicago, Ill.,: Argus Communications Co., 1969, p. 167.)

Two Major Reasons For Our Weaknesses

The scriptures reveal that there are two major reasons for our weaknesses. One purpose is to develop within our character the traits which are the exact opposite of the weakness so that we will achieve strength where we were weak. The other purpose is to draw us closer to the Lord. These are two of the most exciting ideas we can find in scripture. As we come to understand the workings of these two goals, we will learn to view our weaknesses as the Lord does; that is, as the very doors through which we may pass to enter into the acquisition of strength and increased spirituality.

One of the most important revelations regarding weaknesses was recorded by Moroni. Let us first review his words and then consider some of their wonderful implications.

> And when I had said this, the Lord spake unto me, saying: Fools mock, but they shall mourn; and my grace is sufficient for the meek, that they shall take no advantage of your weakness;
>
> And if men come unto me I will show unto them their weakness. I give unto men weakness that they may be humble; and my grace is sufficient for all men that humble themselves before me; for if they humble themselves before me, and have faith in me, then will I make weak things become strong unto them. (Ether 12:26-27.)

We cannot correct a weakness which we do not recognize. Therefore, a major part of the growth process is discovering our weaknesses and then admitting to ourselves and to God the areas where we need his help. It was for this reason that he promised to "show" us our weaknesses when we try to come closer to him.

How many times have we been motivated to overcome a weakness, or to seek a closer relationship with the Lord, only to end up frustrated by an increased awareness of our failures? That can be a very perplexing situation unless we understand that such an awareness is a blessing, and that it is necessary before we can do the things required to find the Lord, who is anxiously and joyously waiting to welcome us on the other side of the doors of our weaknesses. We can only approach him through the truth, and this must include the awareness of our own condition before him. To sensitize our spiritual awareness of areas needing personal growth is one of the major roles assigned to the Holy Ghost. (John 16:8, 13.)

If we were sufficiently humble on our own, we could be much closer to the Lord than most of us are. Therefore, knowing the natural tendency which we have to take pride in being strong and self-sufficient, God lovingly gives us weaknesses which we cannot overcome all by ourselves, so that we will find humility, recognize our need for his help, and then be drawn closer to him as we learn to rely upon him for strength.

> And *because thou hast seen thy weakness thou shalt be made strong,* even unto the sitting down in the place which I have prepared in the mansions of my Father (Ether 12:37).

Recognizing our weaknesses, then, is the beginning of our discovery of our need for Christ as Savior and Deliverer from those weaknesses. This process will lead us to the humility which is necessary to draw from the Lord the strength and grace to "be made strong" in his sight. Indeed, that is one of the main reasons that he gives us weaknesses.

> . . . I give unto men weakness *that they may be humble;* and my grace is sufficient for all men that humble themselves before me; for if they humble themselves before me, and have faith in me, then will I make weak things become strong unto them (Ether 12:27).

Notice how Moroni emphasized that the purpose of our weaknesses is to bring us closer to the Lord or, as Paul expressed it, "that the power of Christ may rest upon me" (2 Cor. 12:9). Moroni did not say that it was enough just to be humble. Humility alone will not suffice. What he said was that we must be humble *before* Christ as our Master and Savior. We become properly humble "before him" when we recognize and admit that we cannot, by ourselves, cure our own spiritual infirmities, overcome every weakness on our own, or save ourselves; and when we admit how very much we need his power in our life.

We all feel discouraged when we fail in our efforts to overcome bad habits and weaknesses. That is a natural reaction, but such experiences can easily cause us to lose faith in ourselves. Nevertheless, though it is a painful door through which to pass, such realizations can give birth to a deeper and far more effective faith in Jesus Christ, which is where we should have been focusing our faith in the first place. It is when we learn to replace faith and trust in our own power with faith and trust in the Savior's unlimited power that we move at last from weakness to strength.

> Nevertheless, the Lord God showeth us our weakness *that we may know that it is by his grace,* and his great condescensions unto the children of men, that we have power to do these things (Jacob 4:7).

The Lord's promise to each of us who properly humble ourselves before him, and place our faith in him more than in ourselves, is that he will perform within us the miracle which converts our weakness into strength.

> . . . for if they humble themselves before me, and have faith in me, *then will I make weak things become strong unto them* (Ether 12:27).

> Behold, and hearken, O ye elders of my church, saith the Lord your God, even Jesus Christ, your advocate, *who knoweth the weakness of man* and how to succor them who are tempted (D&C 62:1).

> . . . some of you are guilty before me, but *I will be merciful unto your weakness* (D&C 38:14).

> . . . I will be merciful unto you; *he that is weak among you hereafter shall be made strong* (D&C 50:16).

> . . . the tender mercies of the Lord are over all those whom he hath chosen, because of their faith, *to make them mighty* even unto the power of deliverance (1 Ne. 1:20).

How marvelous it is to know that our weakest traits can become our greatest strengths! Jesus has promised that there is no weakness holding us enslaved which is stronger than his power to free us. He who said that "all power is given unto me in heaven and in earth" (Matt. 28:18) has promised us that his grace "is sufficient for *all* men that humble themselves before" him. The key to gaining the power of his grace which will make our strength perfect is to recognize our need for him, and then to come to him with humility, trust and faith. How can we doubt that he who changed water into wine cannot change our weaknesses into strengths as he has promised?

Of course, the Savior's promise of grace does not mean that there will be no effort required on our part. The Lord always requires of us to do all that we can do. (See 2 Ne. 25:23; D&C 123:17.) The promise of Christ to convert our weaknesses into strengths, then, is not that he will do everything for us, but that as we struggle, he will amplify, magnify and increase the power of our efforts so that through him and with him we can achieve the victory we could never have found on our own.

The victories which we obtain by ourselves may be limited, but what the Lord undertakes to do will always be complete and whole, or, as James said, "perfect and entire, wanting nothing" (James 1:4). And, as the Savior promised, "he that is faithful shall be made strong *in every place*" (D&C 66:8).

The Apostle Paul had a weakness which proved to be such an aggravation that he referred to it as a "thorn in the flesh" (2 Cor. 12:7). Three times he pleaded with God to remove this affliction from him; each time his request was denied.

Paul, like us, wanted to be comfortable. But the Lord had more important things in mind—he wanted Paul to become great by becoming humble, by becoming strong, and by becoming close to him. Paul was given an answer to his prayers that teaches us much about God's purposes in blessing us with weaknesses.

> And he [Christ] said unto me, My grace is sufficient for thee: for my strength is made perfect in weakness. *Most gladly* therefore will I rather glory in my infirmities, *that the power of Christ may rest upon me.*
>
> *Therefore I take pleasure* in infirmities, in reproaches, in necessities, in persecutions, in distresses for Christ's sake: for when I [recognize that I] am weak, then am I [become] strong. (2 Cor. 12:9-10; see also 2 Cor. 11:29-30; D&C 122:7; 2 Ne. 2:2.)

Paul came to understand this paradox well, and his attitude of escape (take it away and let me be comfortable) was changed to one of gratitude and enthusiastic involvement in the challenge. Following his example is not always easy, but is immensely rewarding. So the question before us now is not so much about where we have turned in the past when we felt discouraged and in need of strength, but where will we turn from now on? Will we permit our struggles, weaknesses and discouragements to draw us closer to the Savior, or will we allow the devil to continue to use them to place barriers between us and the Lord?

V
The Power Of God

Nothing Is Impossible

One of the most oft repeated messages through centuries of revealed scripture is that God our Father and Jesus Christ our Savior have possession of "all power" both "in heaven and in earth."

> But the Lord knoweth all things from the beginning; wherefore, he prepareth a way to accomplish all his works among the children of men; for behold, *he hath all power* unto the fulfilling of all his words (1 Ne. 9:6).
>
> . . . the Lord God hath *power to do all things* which are according to his word (Alma 7:8).

It was just prior to the Savior's final departure from Jerusalem that he gave his disciples the great missionary charge to go forth to all nations, teaching his gospel, baptizing, and building the kingdom. At that same time, just before his ascension, Jesus also made two statements regarding his divine and unlimited power. They were almost the last words he spoke, and surely of great significance.

> . . . All power is given unto me in heaven and in earth (Matt. 28:18).

> But ye shall receive power, after that the Holy Ghost is come upon you . . . (Acts 1:8).

Why was it so important to the Lord, as he departed and left the leadership of his worldwide ministry in the hands of his apostles, to change their concept of him from that of a conquered and crucified man to that of a conquering and immortal God of power? It was important because he knew that no believer would dare to rely upon him, or dare to commit his obedience to him, if he were thought to be a god of weakness. As Joseph Smith taught:

> And it is not less necessary that men should have the idea of the existence of the attribute power in the Deity; for unless God had power over all things, and was able by his power to control all things, and thereby deliver his creatures who put their trust in him from the power of all beings that might seek their destruction, whether in heaven, on earth, or in hell, men could not be saved. *But with the idea of the existence of this attribute planted in the mind, men feel as though they had nothing to fear who put their trust in God, believing that he has power to save all who come to him to the very uttermost.* (*Lectures on Faith,* 4:12, p. 43; emphasis added.)

The Savior knew that his disciples would encounter many difficult situations in building the kingdom and in perfecting their individual characters; difficult situations and obstacles which would often surpass their limitations. He wanted them (and us) to know that even though he is in heaven, he still governs the affairs of men, that he has unlimited power with which to influence our circumstances, and that he is willing and able to share that power with us. He uses that infinite power to do whatever is required to "save every man" that is willing to qualify through obedience to his laws and ordinances.

> And he [Christ] received all power, both in heaven and on earth . . . (D&C 93:17).

> . . . *he has all power to save every man* that believeth on his name and bringeth forth fruit meet for repentance (Alma 12:15).

The word, power, occurs over 800 times in scripture! Indeed, the message of God's power, as manifest in the scriptures is such that the word "power" is actually a symbol of the gospel; it is almost synonymous.

> For I am not ashamed of the gospel of Christ: *for it is the power of God* unto salvation to everyone that believeth. . . (Rom. 1:16).

> For our gospel came not unto you in word only, *but also in power,* and in the Holy Ghost, and in much assurance. . . (1 Thes. 1:5).

> The kingdom of God is not in word, but in power (1 Cor. 4:20).

The emphasis of such scriptures is that when we feel incapable of achieving gospel goals, or fulfilling our assignments, when we feel powerless to overcome and conquer our weaknesses and faults, *we are missing out on the power of the gospel*! Surrendering our problems to the Lord—that is, recognizing and admitting how much we need the help of his power added to our own—will focus our faith, and result in a stronger influence from a loving Father and Savior, who already want to use their power for our good.

The Lord delights in placing us in circumstances whereby we may learn for ourselves that our Father and Elder Brother are Gods of unlimited power, and that they are anxious to use that power "in heaven and in earth" in our behalf. The following testimony by Parley P. Pratt provides an example of how God's power can reach out and influence our circumstances, affecting even total strangers if necessary.

> . . . I took leave and entered Hamilton, a flourishing town at the head of Lake Ontario; but my place of destination was Toronto, around on the north side of the lake. If I went by land I would have a circuitous route, muddy and tedious to go on foot. The lake had just opened, and steamers had commenced plying between the two places; two dollars would convey me to Toronto in a few hours, and save some days of laborious walking; but I was an entire stranger in Hamilton, and also in the province; and money I had none. Under these circumstances I pondered what I should do. I had many times received answers to prayer in such matters; but now it seemed hard to exercise faith, because I was among strangers and entirely unknown. *The Spirit seemed to whisper to me to try the Lord, and see if anything was too hard for him, that I might know and trust him under all circumstances.* I retired to a secret place in a forest and prayed to the Lord for money to enable me to cross the lake. I then entered Hamilton and commenced to chat with some of the people. I had not arrived many minutes before I was accosted by a stranger, who inquired my name and where I was going. He also asked me if I did not want some money. I said yes. He then gave me ten dollars and a letter of introduction to John Taylor, of Toronto, where I arrived the same evening. (From the autobiography of Parley P. Pratt, quoted in the 1969-70 Gospel Doctrine Manual, *In His Footsteps Today,* p. 81; emphasis added.)

The Lord has told us repeatedly that NOTHING is impossible for him so that we will understand that the only thing which is impossible is that we could ever become involved in a problem which is too difficult for him to solve. When Abraham and Sarah "were old and well stricken in age" and when it had "ceased to be with Sarah after the manner of women," it was revealed to them that at last Sarah would give birth to the long promised son, Isaac. In response to their surprise that Sarah's long barren, and now aged, womb would finally conceive and bear a son, they were asked, "Is anything too hard for the Lord" (See Gen. 18:9-14). Abraham's faith and trust in God's power is often cited as an example toward which we should strive.

> And being not weak in faith, he considered not his own body now dead, when he was about an hundred years old, neither yet the deadness of Sara's womb:
>
> He staggered not at the promise of God through unbelief; but was strong in faith, giving glory to God;
>
> *And being fully persuaded that, what he had promised, he was able also to perform.* (Rom. 4:19-21.)

When we find ourselves faced with difficult circumstances, or obstacles which seem impossible to resolve, we should separate our needs from the emotional anxiety which blocks our faith, and ask ourselves: "Are my problems too hard for the Lord? Do I believe that he has the power to help me solve this problem or not?" Nothing is too hard for God if we will only cooperate with him and allow him to work his great power for our good as he has promised. (See Rom. 8:28; D&C 90:24; 100:15.) "For with God nothing shall be impossible" (Luke 1:37).

> With men it is impossible, but not with God: for with God all things are possible (Mark 10:27).

> And I know, O Lord, that thou hast all power, and can do whatsoever thou wilt for the benefit of man (Ether 3:4).

Having A Form Of Godliness

Paul described one of the signs of apostasy as being both people and church organizations who have a "form of godliness," but "deny the power thereof" (See 2 Tim. 3:5). When Joseph Smith asked which church he should join, he was forbidden to join any of them, because "they teach for doctrines the commandments of men, having a form of godliness, but they deny the power thereof" (JS-H 19; see also 2 Ne. 28:3-5).

When we are confronted with a challenging situation that appears to be more than we can handle, do we look beyond the horizons of our own ability to the Lord's power and grace, or does our confidence waver while we tremble in fear and doubt? In other words, do we really believe in and claim the power of the gospel, or do we settle for a mere "form of godliness" based on nothing but our own power? The Lord has warned that any person who seeks to build himself up on his own, without the aid of God, will surely fail, and will reveal his own folly.

> And if any man shall seek to build up himself, and seeketh not my counsel, *he shall have no power,* and his folly shall be made manifest (D&C 136:19; see also D&C 3:4).
>
> . . . I would exhort you that ye *deny not the power of God;* for he worketh by power, according to the faith of the children of men, the same today and tomorrow, and forever (Moro. 10:7; see also 2 Ne. 28:26).

God Wants To Share His Power With Us

> If man is to become like Christ, by means of the Holy Spirit, he must begin to partake of the divine truth and power which Jesus possesses. *A major purpose of Christ's mission on earth* was to reveal his glory to man (John 1:14) and *to give man the divine truth and power required* to attain to salvation in the presence of God. (1969-70 Gospel Doctrine Manual, *In His Footsteps Today,* p. 29; emphasis added.)

It has been a precious discovery in my life to find that the Lord is not only able and willing to assist our efforts to overcome our faults and increase our righteousness, but that he is actually anxious to do so. Whereas, before I learned this, I felt reluctant to request help from him, fearing that my own efforts may have been insufficient or unacceptable, I now realize that he truly wants us to come to him for strength. He does not expect us to overcome every weakness and accomplish every requirement of righteous living by the strength of our mortal abilities alone. God's goodness moves him to want our success more than we can want our own success.

> The way of the Lord is strength to the upright . . . (Prov. 10:29).
>
> The Lord will give strength unto his people . . . (Ps. 29:11).

Nephi is famous for his reassuring confirmations of the Lord's eager willingness to endow men with the ability to accomplish their responsibilities.

> . . . I know that the Lord giveth no commandments unto the children of men, save *he shall prepare a way* for them that they may accomplish the thing which he commanded them (1 Ne. 3:7).
>
> And if it so be that the children of men keep the commandments of God he doth *nourish them,* and *strengthen them,* and *provide means* whereby they can accomplish the thing which he has commanded them . . . (1 Ne. 17:3).

The Lord can never "nourish [us], and strengthen [us], and provide means whereby [we] can accomplish the thing which he has commanded [us]" unless we invite him to do so by getting our limitations out of his way. One of the most important verses in the New Testament is the testimony of Paul that the Lord "is able to do exceeding abundantly above all that we [dare to] ask or think, *according to the power that worketh in us*" (Eph. 3:20). The Lord has things planned for our progress and joy that we cannot yet conceive, but notice that his power to work these "exceedingly abundant" blessings in our life is dependent upon, or "according to the power that worketh in us." Thus we can see why it is so important that we choose to let God's power have dominance in our life, instead of trying to achieve everything strictly by our own limited powers.

> Nevertheless, the Lord God showeth us our weakness *that we may know that it is by his grace,* and his great condescensions unto the children of men, *that we have power to do*

> *these things* (Jacob 4:7).

In the Book of Mormon we are told of the misfortune which fell upon the Nephites when they forgot their dependence upon God. Because of "their boastings in their own strength, they were left in their own strength; therefore they did not prosper, but were afflicted and smitten. . . (Hel. 4:13). It is a form of pride to presume that we can adequately perform all gospel duties by virtue of our own abilities and skills alone.[8] But if we will borrow the Lord's strength as he intended, we will have the power to go all the way in accomplishing all things that are required of us.

> He giveth power to the faint; and to them that have no might he increaseth strength (Isa. 40:29).
>
> And Christ hath said: If ye will have faith in me ye shall have power to do whatsoever thing is expedient in me (Moro. 7:33).
>
> And I will give unto him strength such as is not known among men (D&C 24:12).

Paul summarized the endowment of power from Jesus Christ in beautiful and concise words which have inspired millions of disciples to achieve mighty things which they could not have otherwise accomplished. He testified: "I can do all things through Christ which strengtheneth me" (Philip. 4:13). Book of Mormon authors and others also gave expression to the same testimony.

> . . . I know, in the strength of the Lord thou canst do all things (Alma 20:4).

---

[8]This concept is discussed further in chapter nine.

> Yea, I know that I am nothing; as to my strength I am weak; therefore I will not boast of myself, but I will boast of my God, for in his strength I can do all things. . . (Alma 26:12).

> The Lord is my light; the Lord is my strength,
> I know in his might I'll conquer at length.
> My weakness in mercy he covers with power,
> And, walking by faith, I am blest every hour.
> (Hymns, No. 103.)

The faith and power to "do all things" through Jesus Christ is there for all of us, but it is not attained in an instant. Rather, it comes through a natural growth process. We begin where we are, expressing our faith and desire for his power and our willingness and commitment to be in harmony with his will. Then, as we gain experience with his grace in small things, our capacity will grow to greater and greater accomplishments, until we truly "can do all things" through and for Christ.

Expanding ourselves to do mighty things through the power and grace of Jesus Christ is not just a pleasant option—it is a commandment. Paul, for example, admonished: "Finally, my brethren, be strong in the Lord, and in the power of his might" (Eph. 6:10). Having so commanded, he prayed for the saints of his time (as we should pray today) to receive this mighty endowment of power through the grace of Jesus Christ and Heavenly Father.

> For this cause I bow my knees unto the Father of our Lord Jesus Christ,
>
> That he would grant you, according to the riches of his glory, to be *strengthened with might* by his Spirit in the inner man. (Eph. 3:14, 16.)

While the Lord is anxious to share his power with us, the endowment of power through his grace is not intended to substitute for the effort which man is expected to make with his own abilities. Rather, it is intended to add thereto, thereby enabling us to proceed forward (and upward) past the point of the limitations of our own natural capacities. Stephen Covey has provided a beautiful summary of this concept in the following words:

> Furthermore, we can't fully overcome these habits and impacted tendencies by ourselves. Our own resolves, our own will, our own effort—all this is necessary but is not sufficient. We need the transforming power of the Savior, born of faith in him and his atoning sacrifice and of entering into a contract with him. In such a contract, made in ordinance work and in private prayer, we covenant, or promise, or witness to take upon ourselves his name and to keep his commandments. He, in turn, promises us to give us his spirit, *which, if we are true to our promises, will renew and strengthen and transform us. In this way we combine our power with the power of the Almighty.* (Stephen R. Covey, *Spiritual Roots of Human Relations,* S.L.C., Utah: Deseret Book Co., 1970, p. 93; emphasis added.)

> The eyes of your understanding being enlightened; that ye may know . . . what is the exceeding greatness of his power to us-ward who believe, according to the working of his mighty power. . . (Eph. 1:18-19; see also Col. 1:27-29).

Only We Can Limit God's Power Toward Us

We have learned that God our Father and his Son, Jesus Christ, have "all power" both in heaven and on earth, and that nothing is impossible for them. We have learned that they are anxious to assist our best efforts with an endowment of power which can enable us to accomplish great and mighty things far beyond our own limited powers. We have also learned that God is not limited by our personal abilities, nor is he limited by the restrictions of our circumstances which so often seem to shout failure to us when we try to be realistic. There is, however, one important power which even

God does not have.

> He has all power in heaven and earth, but the power to do his work in man against man's will, he has not got (Johann Tauler, quoted in *Prayer Can Change Your Life,* 17th Ed., Englewood Cliffs, N.J.: Prentice-Hall, Inc., 1965, p. 244).

In other words, the only thing which can limit God's power in our lives is our own agency. If we choose to ignore his power or to disbelieve that he would be willing to share it with us, then he cannot endow us. His grace and power in our life is not only dependent upon our faithfulness and worthiness, but also upon our acceptance.

> For I am God, and mine arm is not shortened; and I will show miracles, signs, and wonders, *unto all those who believe on my name* (D&C 35:8).
>
> For behold . . . I am a God of miracles; and I will show unto the world that I am the same yesterday, today, and forever; *and I work not among the children of men save it be according to their faith* (2 Ne. 27:23).

If we could comprehend the infinite and perfect love with which he yearns to help us, we would "tremble under his power" and be far more anxious to put our life in harmony with his will that we might, through him, "be made strong" (see D&C 52:17).

> . . . the Lord is able to do all things according to his will, for the children of men, *if* it so be that they exercise faith in him. . . (1 Ne. 7:12).
>
> When Jesus sought to give others the living attributes and powers of the Spirit that lead to eternal life, he was restricted by their unbelief (1969-70 Gospel Doctrine Manual, *In His Footsteps Today*, p. 31).

VI
Overcoming

Meeting Conflict: Our Duty

As a church, we profess to believe in facing our conflicts and enduring in our battles with sin and weakness until we achieve victory. "For it must needs be, that there is an opposition in all things. If not so . . . righteousness could not be brought to pass. . ." (2 Ne. 2:11.) ". . . we have endured many things, and hope to be able to endure all things (Articles of Faith, No. 13).

Unfortunately, many of us do not care to face opposition and "endure all things," so we waste our time, emotion, and mental capacity in a futile attempt to bypass the inevitable conflict between good and evil. Speaking of those who will inherit the celestial kingdom, Jesus said they would only be those saints who "shall overcome all things" (D&C 76:60). It is impossible to imagine a person in the celestial kingdom who is still a slave to his weaknesses or bad habits. Let us mark well the necessity of facing and conquering every circumstance, temptation, and weakness which could otherwise prevent our exaltation.

Heavenly Father did not send us here to seek a life of comfort, but to live a progressive life of challenges and growth. "And God blessed them, and God said unto them . . . replenish the earth, and *subdue it: and have dominion* . . ." (Gen. 1:28). To subdue the earth means to conquer and bring into subjection the elements of nature, including our own mortal bodies. To "have dominion" is to have control over the circumstances of life, rather than being controlled by them.

People who are progressing toward the heights of celestial life will arrive there by subduing their "natural man" and by gaining dominion over all forms of inferiority, sin, and selfishness. People who are regressing through the compromises of telestial life will arrive there by default because they have allowed inferiority, sin, or selfishness to have dominion over their lives.

In his lecture, "As a Man Thinketh," James Allen said that "as a progressive and evolving being, man is where he is that he may learn that he may grow: and as he learns the spiritual lesson which any circumstance contains for him, it passes away and gives place to other circumstances." This statement should clarify why some problems and habits seem to never go away. When we learn to look for the lessons our conflicts and challenges can teach us, when we face them courageously, and do battle until we overcome, we may be surprised how quickly those circumstances vanish, making way for new experiences.

Overcoming the forces which pull us down into the comfort of mediocrity and the wickedness of compromise is not only our duty to God, but one that we owe to ourselves.

> . . . let us labor diligently; for if we should cease to labor, we should be brought under condemnation; *for we have a labor to perform whilst in this tabernacle of clay, that we may conquer the enemy of all righteousness,* and rest our souls in the kingdom of God (Moro. 9:6).

Pretending We Can't Change

Through the power of Jesus Christ we can overcome virtually every problem confronting us. Unfortunately, however, many of us try to justify our weaknesses and sins by insisting that we are helpless before them. How often we say, "I can't help it; it's just the way I am." This rationalization may be soothing to a mistreated conscience, but is absolutely the wrong way to solve our problems.

In a talk delivered at a BYU fireside on March 5, 1978, Elder Boyd K. Packer of the Quorum of the Twelve Apostles said, "If someone is heavily involved in perversion (or any sin), it becomes very important to him to believe that it is incurable" (*Devotional Speeches of the Year*, Provo, Utah: Brigham Young University Press, 1978, p. 35). Sterling W. Sill said that "no one can overcome a temptation that he doesn't want to resist (*Making The Most Of Yourself*, S.L.C., Utah: Bookcraft, Inc., 1971, p. 20). And someone else said, "There is never any real barrier to your success but your own weakness of purpose and lack of commitment."

> O ye wicked and perverse generation, why hath Satan got such great hold upon your hearts? *Why will ye yield yourselves unto him that he may have power over you,* to blind your eyes, that ye will not understand the words which are spoken, according to their truth? (Alma 10:25.)

In their book, *Prayer Can Change Your Life,* Doctor William R. Parker and Elaine St. Johns discuss rationalization, and some of the tricks we play in our minds to convince ourselves that we are still "okay," even though we have allowed a problem to have dominion over us.

> *This will to fail is more common than most of us would believe,* and extremely easy to fall into because, in odd ways, there is a certain amount of success guaranteed the man who wills to fail.
>
> One of the chief rewards for not trying is that, while you never know how high you might have climbed, you are never, never forced to face your limitations. (17th Ed., Englewood Cliffs, N.J.: Prentice-Hall, Inc. 1965, p. 27; emphasis added.)

It may be difficult for us to seriously entertain the idea that the "natural man," or carnal part of us might actually be playing this deadly game of pretense with us. But it is important that we examine ourselves honestly for that possibility. So many times our favorite weaknesses and sins are lingering on because, in spite of the guilt we feel, we are somehow more comfortable with the pain that they cause than we are with the idea of changing and growing. After all, if we do not have some of the "will to fail" in us, if we are not deliberately or subconsciously clinging to our faulty behavior, then why do our faults persist?

> While changing one's life from evil to good is admittedly not easy, we cannot emphasize too strongly that every person endowed with normal faculties can do it. Elder Richard L. Evans has said:
>
> ". . . in life no road can be retraveled just as once it was. We can't begin where we were. But we can begin where we are, and in an eternity of existence, this is a reassuring fact. *There is virtually nothing that a man cannot turn away from if he really wants to . . . There is virtually no habit that he cannot give up if he sincerely sets his will to do so. . .*"
>
> *Setting the will is the key.* There must be resoluteness and determination. The will to do must be strong and kept strenghtened. Napolean is said to have coined the phrase: "He who fears being conquered is sure of defeat." (Spencer W. Kimball, *The Miracle of Forgiveness*, S.L.C., Utah: Bookcraft, Inc., 1969, pp.175-176; emphasis added.)

Just how much desire do we have for change? How much is it worth to us to discard our lesser self for the real person waiting inside? What price are we willing to pay? How long are we going to allow Satan to deceive us through the comfort of mediocrity? No matter how long we have tried and failed, no matter how deep our transgression or weakness is rooted, there is absolutely nothing that the Savior's power cannot overcome when we allow him to join in our battles.

> Faith in Jesus Christ consists of complete reliance on Him. As God, He has infinite power, intelligence, and love. *There is no human problem beyond His capacity to solve.* Because He descended below all things (see D&C 122:8), He knows how to help us rise above our daily difficulties . . . *There is no evil which He cannot arrest.* ("Jesus Christ: Our Savior and Redeemer," Ezra Taft Benson, *Ensign,* November 1983, p. 8; emphasis added.)

> In abandoning evil, transforming lives, changing personalities, molding characters or remolding them, *we need the help of the Lord, and we may be assured of it if we do our part. The man who leans heavily upon his Lord becomes the master of self and can accomplish anything he sets out to do,* whether it be to secure the brass plates, build a ship, overcome a habit, or conquer a deep-seated transgression.
>
> He who has greater strength than Lucifer, he who is our fortress and our strength, can sustain us in times of great temptation. While the Lord will never forcibly take anyone out of sin or out of the arms of the tempters, he exerts his Spirit to induce the sinner to do it with divine assistance. *And the man who yields to the sweet influence and pleadings of the Spirit and does all in his power to stay in a repentant attitude is guaranteed protection, power, freedom and joy.* (Spencer W. Kimball, *The Miracle of Forgiveness,* S.L.C., Utah: Bookcraft, Inc., 1969, p. 176; emphasis added.)

As the repentance process begins, our resolves are firm and promises are made. Very often, however, resolves weaken, and the promises we made are broken. Even though the Lord is disappointed when we break our word to him, he is not so much concerned about the broken promise as he is about what we learned from our failure. While Satan would convince us otherwise, as long as we maintain a sincerely "repentant attitude," we will find the Lord willing and anxious to assist us.

The Starting Point: "A Willing Mind"

We have learned that we came to earth to grow through encounters with conflict. We have also learned that it is our duty to face challenges and make choices, that "flight" instead of "fight" only prolongs our battles. We have discovered that the more we learn about the Savior's life and power, the greater our confidence will be in following his footsteps. We may attempt to wage our battles at the surface level of outward behavior, using only our mortal will power and strength, or we may invite the Lord to be a part of our struggle, and experience the joy of having him change our hearts and natures, so that our faults are removed from the inside out. And we have learned that there is absolutely no fault, weakness, or bad habit that is beyond the power of his redeeming grace.

But where do we start? How do we find success in overcoming our faults where we have failed so many times before? How do we get the words off the pages of this book and into the fiber of our everyday life? The inspired words of Helen Wodehouse and the two scriptures which follow, identify the starting point for all change in human behavior: simply "a willing mind."

> We think we must climb to a certain height of goodness before we can reach God. But He says not "at the end of the way you may find me;" He says "I am the way; I am the road under your feet, the road that begins just as low down as you happen to be."
>
> If we are in a hole then the Way begins in the hole. The moment we set our face in the same direction as His, we are walking with God. (Quoted by William R. Parker & Elaine St. Johns, *Prayer Can Change Your Life,* 17th Ed., Englewood Cliffs, N.J.: Prentice-Hall, Inc., 1965, pp. 244-245.)

> For if there be first *a willing mind,* it is accepted according to that [which] a man hath, and not according to that [which] he hath not (2 Cor. 8:12).

> Yea, I say unto you, come and fear not, and lay aside every sin, which easily doth beset you, which doth bind you down to destruction, yea, come and go forth, and *show unto your God that ye are willing to repent* of your sins and enter into a covenant with him to keep his commandments. . . (Alma 7:15).

God does not require nor expect perfection from us as we initiate improvements in our lives. He only requires that we start from where we are, "according to that [which] a man hath," without condemning ourselves for our limitations, "according to that [which] he hath not," and that we be "willing" to work with the abilities we do have, even if it is no more than "a willing mind." In return for this commitment, the Lord has promised to accept us—even with our temporary limitations—and not reject or refuse us because we do not yet have the perfected feelings and habits of obedience which can only be produced with time.

When we take a stand, when we "voice our choice," we must not allow the decision to depend upon our emotional commitment, because in many cases, our true feelings will be exactly opposite our mental choice. Many of the problems we encounter in overcoming our faults come from trying to choose with our *emotions* instead of our *will.* We cannot expect our feelings to obey our will the instant we make a choice. As Doctor Maxwell Maltz explained, "Feelings cannot be voluntarily made to order, or turned on or off like a faucet" (*Psychocybernetics,* Wilshire Book Ed., Englewood Cliffs, N.J.: Prentice-Hall, 1960, p. 219).

President Kimball has warned of the danger of allowing our decisions and commitments to depend upon the way we *feel,* instead of on what we know is right.

> Emotions must not wholly determine decisions, but the mind and the heart, strengthened by fasting and prayer and serious consideration, will give one a maximum chance of . . . happiness (*Marriage,* S.L.C., Utah: Deseret Book Co., 1978, p. 32).

> We must not let the attractions of the moment bring disaster for the eternities (*The Miracle of Forgiveness,* S.L.C., Utah: Bookcraft, Inc., 1969, p., 246).

The turning point in my return to the Church came when I finally surrendered my life to the Lord. But I had a serious misconception. I thought that perhaps my commitment was too weak, or that there was something wrong with me because, in spite of my sincerity, my emotions did not immediately follow my mental choice. Mentally, I had committed myself to repent and turn to the Lord "with all my heart," but emotionally I found myself being pulled back to my old ways by a lifetime of improper habits.

Mentally, I did not want to go back to my sins, yet I felt certain God would reject me because my weaknesses would not allow me to live perfect from the moment of my commitment and because my inner feelings were not yet in harmony with my intent. I believe everyone has experienced this problem. Perhaps, for example, we really want to forgive someone, but our feelings just won't let go of the hurt. Or, perhaps we have resolved to conquer a bad habit, but when the confrontations arrive, our feelings of commitment are weakened by our habitual desire for the sin. Then, as we waver, we feel confused, unworthy, hypocritical, and discouraged.

I did not understand that the Lord always allows us time to grow, and that he never rejects us simply because we could only begin with "a willing mind." I had not yet realized that changes in our feelings come only after changes in our actions. Eventually I learned that it is futile to demand the feeling before the act, and that it is self-defeating foolishness to postpone the commitment to right actions while we wait for our feelings to motivate us. When we choose properly with our will, the Lord will work within us to help the proper feelings come (see Philip. 2:13).

Why, then, is it so important to recognize "a willing mind" as the starting point for all growth? Because that is really the only point at which we can begin. And because it is a point at which virtually anyone can begin. True, at the time of our initial commitment, we may not have the ability to *feel* repentant, or to *feel* forgiving, or to *feel* humble, or to *feel* whatever it is that we are trying to achieve, but no matter how discouraged or hopeless we feel, in spite of our feelings, we can always express a mental "willingness" to our Father in Heaven.

The Lord's grace is so kind and merciful that if even our mental willingness is weak and wavering, even if we can only muster that tiny particle of desire described in Alma chapter 32, we can call upon the Lord to reinforce our vacillating choice! Consider the encouraging words of Boyd K. Packer of the Council of the Twelve Apostles, as he spoke to a group at BYU on February 21, 1978:

> But you yourself can call upon a power that can renew your body. *You can draw upon a power that will reinforce your will . . .*
>
> Oh, if I could only convince you that you are a son or a daughter of Almighty God! *You have a righteous, spiritual power—an inheritance that you have hardly touched.* You have an Elder Brother who is your Mediator, your Physician. (*Devotional Speeches of the Year,* Provo, Utah: Brigham Young University Press, 1978, p. 40; emphasis added.)

Once we voice our choice, once we convenant through "an act of the will," that we are truly "willing" to change, even though we realize we won't be able to overcome all the fault by our efforts alone, then Christ will fill the gap between our need and our ability, and through his grace, he will add to our limitations all the additional power we need to make the changes.

> . . . for we know that it is by grace that we are saved, after all we can do (2 Ne. 25:23).
>
> . . . let us cheerfully do all things that lie in our power; and then may we stand still, with the utmost assurance, to see the salvation of God, and for his arm to be revealed (D&C 123:17).

How Christ's Victories Give Us Confidence

During his last night in mortality, Jesus prophecied, "In the world ye shall have tribulation: but be of good cheer; I have overcome the world" (John 16:33). Why should the fact that Christ has overcome all the evil and weaknesses of mortality bring us "good cheer" as we struggle to overcome our tribulations? Because what he has done, he can teach us to do. "For I am able to make you holy. . ." (D&C 60:7).

We have been assured that no worthy member of the Church ever need suffer enslavement to sins or weaknesses, for "the kingdom is given you of the Father, *and power to overcome all things which are not ordained of Him*" (D&C 50:35). "But I have tried everything I know to overcome my faults—and still I fail," we may cry. Jesus Christ never fails. Therefore, if we have failed in our effort to overcome a sin or a weakness, it is because we have not fully made him our partner. It is because we have relied more upon our power than his.

Paul said, "though we walk in the flesh [mortality], we do not war after the flesh. . ." (2 Cor. 10:3). This means that those who rely on Christ to help them overcome their faults do not place their faith and dependence solely upon the human techniques of behavioral control. For "your faith should not stand in the wisdom of men, but in the power of God" (1 Cor. 2:5). Paul continues: "For the weapons of our warfare are not carnal, but MIGHTY through God to the pulling down of strongholds" (2 Cor. 10:4).

> Someone has said "the difference between a man of weakness and one of power lies not in the strength of the personal will, *but in that focus of consciousness which represents their states of knowledge."*
>
> Whatever you give your attention to, is the thing that governs your life. *Attention is the key.* Your free will lies in the directing of your attention. *Whatever you steadfastly direct your attention to, will come into your life and dominate it.* (Emmet Fox, *The Sermon On The Mount,* N.Y., N.Y.: Harper & Row, p. 109; emphasis added.)

Perhaps we have tried and failed a thousand times. As long as our past failures are the focus of our attention, we will continue to fail. As long as we continue to sow thoughts of fear, doubt, and lack of confidence about our abilities to overcome, that is precisely the result we will reap. On the other hand, when we focus our thoughts, faith, and attention on the fact that Jesus has already overcome every problem we can possibly face, then we can, through the miracle of his grace, be endowed with the knowledge and the strength to overcome all our difficulties.

The following quote clarifies the vital difference between the futility of trying to overcome our faults through *behavioral control* alone, and the total victory which comes as we allow Christ to remove our unworthy desires by actually changing our inner nature.

> Now in the gospel, in a sense, there are two fundamental breakdowns. . . There is what we refer to as "the doctrine of Christ," and then there is what we refer to as the moral and ethical principles.
>
> Now, *it is in "the doctrine of Christ" that the power comes.* And because of the power that can flow in a personal relationship with the Lord; giving our lives to Him, serving Him with all of our hearts; through that power, through the heavenly element of the Holy Ghost, we will acquire a celestial dimension of moral and ethical character.
>
> But somewhere along the line we come into the Church and we get a testimony, but we get "caught up" in a kind of

> humanistic approach to solving our personal problems, to changing our behavior. If we get caught up in the approach of hacking away on the moral and ethical principles, we can never, worlds without end, go above and beyond a terrestrial dimension of character in our lives.
>
> But if we accept the Lord and we're filled with His Spirit and we know that *He is the source of the power we need to solve all of our problems,* then the natural acruement to us will be to acquire a kind of honesty, a kind of patience, a kind of love, a kind of integrity that is of a celestial nature. . .
>
> Some of the time I am troubled in my heart when I see men and women who approach the gospel almost as though it is simply a moral and an ethical system. It is all of that, but it is much, much more . . . for finally, it is only He who can change human nature. *Oh, it is true, we can change human behavior, but changing human behavior is a lot different than changing human nature. And only the blood of Christ can place you and I [sic] in a position to have our nature changed.* (George W. Pace, cassette recording, *Developing A Personal Relationship With The Savior,* S.L.C., Utah: Covenant Recordings, Inc., 1979; emphasis added.)

We may battle long and hard to control our behavior, but such a surface battle only deals with the symptoms of our problems. The real source of our faults lies within us, in the carnal and "natural man" part of us. It is there, within our own hearts, that we find the real enemy. It is there, within the depths of our souls, that Jesus Christ is "mighty in battle." ". . . inasmuch as ye are humble and faithful and call upon my name, *behold, I will give you the victory*" (D&C 104:82). "And they all cried with one voice, saying . . . the Spirit of the Lord Omnipotent . . . has wrought a mighty change in us, or in our hearts, that we have no more disposition to do evil, but to do good continually" (Mosiah 5:2; see also Mosiah 4:2-3).

After The Starting Point—What Next?

I remember how confused I was when I finally discovered my need for the Savior to become a part of my personal, day-to-day life. After more than thirty years of trying (but failing) to do everything right by my own strength and power alone, I didn't know how to bring the Savior's grace into my life. I felt ignorant and blind to find that after being "active in the church" all my life, I knew almost nothing about Jesus Christ. "Having [my] understanding darkened, being alienated from the life of God through the ignorance that [was in me], because of the blindness of [my] heart" (Eph. 4:18), I had missed the very heart and core of the gospel, "the doctrine of Christ!"

I had begun my repentance with "an act of the will," but what was I to expect next? I wanted someone to tell me exactly what to do and how to do it, but the guidance I needed came through study and the inspiration of the Holy Ghost. I still marvel as I remember how Heavenly Father and the Savior welcomed me with open arms and taught me, step by step, exactly what I needed to do and what I needed to become—as fast or as slow as I was able to follow.

During my transition from spiritual blindness and self-willed independence to submission and victory through Christ, I learned five principles which helped me continue my growth beyond the starting point of my "act of the will."

1. It is not sinful or wicked to be tempted.

The fact that evil appeals to us, or tempts us, does not prove that we are unworthy. It only verifies the fact that we are mortal. James said, "Blessed is the man that endureth temptation. . ." (James 1:12). Nowhere do the scriptures say, or even hint, "Blessed is the person who never feels temptation." There is no such person. Everyone is tempted by evil, including the Savior, who remained perfectly sinless. Once we accept this truth and stop letting our emotions condemn us for every temptation that appeals to our mortal self, we become free to overcome our temptations in a new and wonderful way.

2. My temptations are separate from me.

Temptations come from Satan, not from us. They belong to this mortal world and are not part of us unless we choose to accept them as such. Our sins and temptations are much easier to resist when we learn to regard them as part of the "carnal nature," instead of a part of ourselves. Then it becomes "I" resisting "it," instead of "I" resisting "me."

When temptations arouse our desires, it is helpful to think of them as winds from Satan, merely blowing past us. They cannot affect us unless we decide to reach out and make them part of our lives. This concept of separation adds so much power to our ability to resist that we can actually say to ourselves, and mean it, "Yes, that might be fun, (or feel good, etc.), BUT IT IS NOT WORTH IT TO ME!"

3. Keep an honest, detailed, day-by-day record of temptations, victories, and failures.

I have suggested this to many people, and it is always astonishing what this simple accounting does for one's confidence. At one point I recorded ninety-four confrontations with a specific temptation within a twenty-eight day period. I was astounded! I had no idea that I was being tempted that much. No wonder I was having trouble overcoming my bad habit. This was not mere temptation, it was all-out war!

During those four weeks, I was able to record eighty victories over the habit. Eighty successes out of ninety-four temptations. Of course, I was sorry for the fourteen failures, but I gained such strength and joy from my eighty victories, that my confidence and hope grew by leaps and bounds. By keeping score I could see that I was winning. The awareness and confidence I gained from this simple score-keeping enabled me to resist temptations that previously would have signaled certain failure.

4. Use the power of accumulation.

The difficulty in overcoming our bad habits lies in the power of the principle of accumulation. Repeated choices for evil establish a pattern, an inclination of mental and emotional response. In other words, repetition of sin causes our brain and body to acquire mental and physical needs. These needs cause us to respond to our temptations and frustrations in patterned ways.

Along comes a time when something motivates us to repent. Then, after a short attempt to change, we find ourselves bound by the strength of our past habits. In spite of our best intentions, we find ourselves falling back into the old patterns, and we become confused and discouraged. Our self-confidence is damaged and our self-image is diminished. Our relationship with Heavenly Father is weakened. Often, our will to try is crippled. What we are experiencing is the accumulated power of hundreds of past decisions for wrong. It is not reasonable to think we can simply erase our past by one or two choices to the contrary, but we often expect to. It requires genuine determination to swim against the stream of our past decisions with only the strength of a few new choices, but we have been promised that it can be done—if our intent is sincere, and if we are committed to continue the battle no matter how long it takes, and especially if we are humble enough to allow the Lord to join our battle by lending us his strength.

The power of accumulation can work *for* us just as it works against us. "That which we persist in doing becomes easier for us to do; not that the nature of the thing itself is changed, but that our power to do is increased" (Heber J. Grant, *Conference Report,* April 1901, p. 63). Understanding that it was the process of accumulation that got us into slavery in the first place will help to free us. Instead of expecting to erase old habits with the simple utterance of a new resolve, we use the power of accumulation for our good, by replacing the bad habit with a good one. "Be not overcome of evil, but overcome evil with good" (Rom. 12:21).

Elder Boyd K. Packer explained our need to "replace" bad habits, instead of simply trying to erase them, in an address at BYU on February 21, 1978:

> Do not try merely to discard a bad habit or a bad thought. Replace it. *When you try to eliminate a bad habit, if the spot where it used to be is left open it will sneak back and crawl again into that empty space. It grew there; it will struggle to stay there.* When you discard it, fill up the spot where it was. Replace it with something good. Replace it with unselfish thoughts, with unselfish acts. Then, if an evil habit or addiction tries to return, it will have to fight for attention. Sometimes it may win. Bad thoughts often have to be evicted a hundred times, or a thousand. But if they have to be evicted ten thousand times, never surrender to them. You are in charge of you. I repeat, *it is very, very difficult to eliminate a bad habit just by trying to discard it. Replace it.* Read in Matthew chapter 12, verses 43 to 45, the parable of the empty house. There is a message in it for you. (*Devotional Speeches Of The Year,* Provo, Utah: Brigham Young University Press, 1978, p. 39; emphasis added.)

5. Avoid tempting situations.

> And now I say unto you, all you that are desirous to follow the voice of the good shepherd, *come ye out from the wicked, and be ye separate,* and touch not their unclean things. . . (Alma 5:57).

In the book of Proverbs we are told that a "prudent man" learns to anticipate and avoid the places, people, situations, and influences which contribute to his weakness and temptations. On the other hand, the foolish person moves right into the damaging environment and falls. "A prudent man forseeth the evil, and hideth himself: but the simple pass on, and are punished" (Prov. 22:3).

> In abandoning sin one . . . should avoid the places and circumstances where the sin occurred, for these could most readily breed it again. He must abandon the people with whom the sin was committed. He may not hate the persons involved, but he must avoid them and everything associated with the sin. He must dispose of all letters, trinkets, and things which will remind him of the 'old days' and the 'old times.' He must forget addresses, telephone numbers, people, places and situations from the sinful past, and build a new life. *He must eliminate anything which would stir the old memories.* (Spencer W. Kimball, *The Miracle Of Forgiveness,* S.L.C., Utah: Bookcraft, Inc., 1969, p. 171-172; emphasis added.)

The "Mighty Change"

We have learned that we cannot, either by "iron-jawed will power," or by behavioral techniques and self-improvement programs alone, change the nature of our hearts and dispositions. We may do much good in terms of controlling our behavior, and that is the right place to start. But until we allow Jesus Christ to take over the affairs of our life, so that he has permission to alter our hearts, we will suffer a continual struggle between the desires of our flesh and the will of our spirit.

> The point of the scriptures is that Christ is great, infinitely greater than any human. But Christ is also the way: as we learn of him, believe in him, accept his prophets and his teachings, we can tread in his footsteps, and *through his power we can come to be as he is.* In the scriptures we learn of him and see the events and decisions and actions of his life. As we study the scriptures, particularly those which tell of his teachings and of the examples of his life, *we can gain increasingly greater knowledge and comprehension of who he is, what he is, and what we may become.* This knowledge is a precious heritage and is our key. (1969-70 Gospel Doctrine Manual, *In His Footsteps Today,* S.L.C., Utah: Deseret Sunday School Union, 1969, p. 6; emphasis added.)

Jesus taught that the inner thoughts, values, emotions, and desires which center in our heart govern our outward behavior (see Luke 6:45). Jeremiah taught that "the heart is deceitful above all things, and desperately wicked. . ." (Jer. 17:9). Anyone who has seriously tried to change a bad habit, overcome a weakness, or conquer an enslaving sin, has felt the resistant protests of his own heart. To continue in this relentless struggle by ourselves is futile because spiritual death can never give life to itself.

The 1969-70 Gospel Doctrine manual emphasized the importance of recognizing our dependence upon Christ. "Only in him can any man find the strength, the power and ability to live a godly life. Only in Christ is there power to transform the human mind and the human heart. . . Only in Jesus Christ can any man . . . be changed from what he is to do the good for which he hopes" (*In His Footsteps Today,* S.L.C., Utah: Deseret Sunday School Union, 1969, p. 4).

> . . . as I said in a former commandment, even so will I fulfill—I will fight your battles (D&C 105:14).
>
> For the Lord your God is he that goeth with you, to fight for you against your enemies, to save you (Deut. 20:4).
>
> . . . and I myself will go with them and be in their midst . . . and nothing shall prevail against them (D&C 32:3).

Having our hearts "established with grace," (Heb. 13:9) is simply God and man working together to achieve by partnership that "mighty change" which could never be achieved by man alone—"that he would grant you, according to the riches of his glory, to be strengthened with might by his Spirit in the inner man" (Eph. 3:16). It is through that wonderful partnership that we are drawn close to both the Father and the Son.

> And according to his faith [in Christ] *there was a mighty change wrought in his heart* . . .

And behold, he preached the word unto your fathers, and a mighty change was also wrought in their hearts. . . (Alma 5:12-13; see also Alma 5:7; 19:33.)

VII
Desires

Above All That We Ask Or Think

Everyone has desires and makes choices. Many of our desires and choices are good because they lead us upward toward God, godliness, and happiness. Many of our choices and desires are bad because they lead us away from God toward misery and spiritual captivity. In either case, God will cause or allow us to receive the consequences as we choose, in accordance with our desires. For some reason, many of us feel guilty about asking the Lord for blessings, and yet he has repeatedly affirmed his promise to respond to our desires. Moroni recorded these plain words:

> Behold, I say unto you that whoso believeth in Christ, doubting nothing, whatsoever he shall ask the Father in the name of Christ it shall be granted him; and *this promise is unto all, even unto the ends of the earth* (Morm. 9:21).

The most frequent repetition of God's promise to respond in accordance with our desires is given in the following familiar words:

> Ask, and it *shall* be given you; seek, and ye shall find; knock, and it shall be opened unto you:
>
> For *everyone* that asketh receiveth; and he that seeketh

> findeth; and to him that knocketh it shall be opened. (Matt. 7:7-8; see also 3 Ne. 27:28-29.)

This divine promise is repeated in scripture so many times that, instead of being impressed by its importance, we let its familiarity cause us to pass over it without realizing what it really means. Notice that the Lord did not say it was only *possible* that we *might* receive according to our desires. He did not say that we would receive if we happened to catch him in a good mood, nor that our receiving depended upon the nature of our request, nor that it depended upon our status in the kingdom. He simply and unequivocally invited us to express our desires by asking.

The Lord chooses his words carefully and deliberately. Consider the difference between saying, "it will be," and the words which he used: "it shall be." The English language is not capable of expressing this idea in a way that would be more inclusive or conclusive. Had the Lord used the word, "will," instead of "shall" in the scripture we just quoted, it would have been a conditional promise instead of the unconditional promise that it is. The word "will" (it *will* be given you, ye *will* find, etc.) is defined as the expression of a "desire or choice, simple futurity" or "probability."

On the other hand, the word "shall" (it *shall* be given you, ye *shall* find, etc.) is used "to express a command," and is "used in laws, regulations, or directives to express what is mandatory and inevitable." (*Webster's Seventh New Collegiate Dictionary,* Springfield, Mass.: G. & C. Merriam Co., 1963.) How much plainer could the Lord be in teaching us that he is going to respond according to our choices and desires?

> Verily, verily, I say unto you, even as you desire of me so it *shall* be done unto you. . . (D&C 11:8).

A proper understanding of this relationship between

God and our desires opens some exciting avenues to the righteous seeker of holiness and perfection. There is so much more that we could achieve by confidently expressing our righteous desires to Heavenly Father. Brigham Young made it clear that most of us are living far below the potential of God's desires to pour down blessings upon us.

> If the Latter-day Saints will *walk up to their privileges* and exercise faith in the name of Jesus Christ and live in the enjoyment of the fullness of the Holy Ghost constantly day by day, there is nothing on the face of the earth that they could ask for that would not be given to them. The Lord is waiting to be very gracious unto this people and to pour out upon them riches, according to the promises he has made through his apostles and prophets. (*Journal of Discourses,* 11:114.)

There are many scriptures which support his view. "I am come that they might have life, and that they might have it more abundantly" (John 10:10). "Yea, I know that God will give liberally to him that asketh" (2 Ne. 4:35; see also James 1:5-6). "But my God shall supply *all your need* according to his riches in glory by Christ Jesus" (Philip. 4:19). In this last and remarkable verse, Paul taught that there is no need too great or too complicated for God; he is willing to supply *all* our needs. When Paul promised God's assistance in supplying "all your need," he had reference to every possible kind of need, both material and spiritual.

> . . . being diligent in keeping the commandments of God at all times; asking for whatsoever things ye stand in need, *both spiritual and temporal;* always returning thanks unto God for whatsoever things ye do receive (Alma 7:23).

Everything which God does is perfect, including the giving of his gifts. Thus, when he gives, it is never an imperfect, incomplete, or partial giving, but abundantly, even "according to his riches in glory." God never experiences a shortage of resources. He has the entire universe at his disposal. Thus it was that Paul challenged us to trust in the benevolence of God, to express our true desires in mighty prayer, and to look "unto him that is able to do exceeding abundantly *above all that we ask or think. . .*" (Eph. 3:20).

Solomon taught: "The fear of the wicked, it shall come upon him: but the desire of the righteous shall be granted" (Prov. 10:24; see also Ps. 37:4). He also said that "the wicked flee when no man pursueth: but *the righteous are bold as a lion*" (Prov. 28:1). How can anyone be that bold in petitioning God? Only with the confidence which comes through personal integrity, for "if our heart condemn us not, then have we confidence toward God" (1 Jn. 3:21). "Happy is he that condemneth not himself in that thing which he alloweth" (Rom. 14:22).

On the other hand, David described the lack of confidence felt by those who cling to their sins and weaknesses when he said, "If I regard [welcome and accept] iniquity in my heart, the Lord will not hear me" (Ps. 66:18). Our relationship with the Lord is crucial to the obtaining of our righteous desires, because when we are close to him we know that he loves us and that it pleases him to bless us (see D&C 76:5).

Hot, Cold, Or Lukewarm?

It is the intensity of our desires that gives them power and influence with God. The more we care about something, the more likely it will be fulfilled and materialize into reality. We know, for example, that the Lord's promise of blessings are most emphatically directed toward those whose desire can be compared to "hunger and thirst" for righteousness, (see 3 Ne. 12:6) two of man's strongest and most frequent desires. The Lord has never promised the same rewards to those who are content with an occasional glance at the menu.

Many of the challenges we face during our mortal probation are designed to test and develop the strength of our righteous desires. Only those righteous desires which will carry us through every possible adversity and sacrifice are strong enough to carry us into exaltation. The Lord seeks from us a total commitment in our desires, yet he is responsive to even the weakest desires of the faltering beginner, which Alma likened to nothing more than a "particle" (Alma 32:27).

While God is merciful to our weaknesses, one thing he will not tolerate is the deliberate refusal to care about anything, because when we are "lukewarm" and satisfied with things just as they are, it is almost impossible to motivate us or work through us. The Lord has warned that he is angered by the empty and hollow person who stands for nothing, seeks nothing, and is content to drift through life exactly as he is, with no desires toward improvement.

> I know thy works, that thou art neither cold nor hot: I would thou wert cold or hot.
>
> So then because thou art lukewarm, and neither cold nor hot, I will spue thee out of my mouth. (Rev. 3:15-16.)

> The worst sin of many people is not that they disbelieve in God; their skepticism is more serious—they just haven't thought about him one way or the other. It isn't that they disbelieve the doctrines of the Church; they just don't care one way or the other. It is one thing to lack faith, but it is still worse to lack interest and enthusiasm. (Sterling W. Sill, The Three I's, *The New Era,* August 1979, p. 7.)

While we are emphasizing the importance of our desires, we must also maintain control and moderation, lest our desires should overrule our agency or judgement of right and wrong. President Kimball has warned, for example, that "we must not let attractions of the moment bring disaster for the eternities" (Spencer W. Kimball, *The Miracle of*

Forgiveness, S.L.C., Utah: Bookcraft, Inc., 1969, p. 246). And, as Alma said, "see that ye bridle all your passions, that ye may be filled with love. . ." (Alma 38:12).

> . . . God, who has created you, on whom you are dependent for your lives and for all that ye have and are, doth grant unto you whatsoever ye ask that is right, in faith, believing that ye shall receive . . . (Mosiah 4:21; see also Enos 1:12; Ps. 145:18-19).

Persistent Prayer

I have found that when I worthily petition the heavens I can count on receiving one of three answers. It may be a "yes," or it may be a "no," but in many cases the answer is, "Let's wait awhile and see if you will trust Me." The Lord did not promise that we would receive according to our desires the very first time we ask. Nor did he promise to open every door the very first time we knock. When we pray properly, that is, with an honest pleading for our desires, tempered with a submissive "thy will be done" attitude, God will answer in the time and in the way that is for our best good. Many times his answers reflect an eternal perspective that is hard for us to perceive because we are so caught up in the desires of our immediate circumstances.

We often ask for things we really wouldn't want if we understood the consequences and the price they carry. Sometimes we ask for things which seem appropriate, but would be harmful because we are not adequately prepared for them. In such cases God's divine love and foreknowledge will mandate that some prerequisites be resolved in our lives before he responds to those desires. And sometimes, when the answers to our prayers are delayed, it is the Lord's way of saying, "Why don't you show me how much you care, so that I may show you how much I care?" Thus it is that Jesus gives emphasis to the importance of persisting in prayer until our lives and circumstances are properly arranged for the wise granting of our requests.

The Lord illustrated the importance of persisting in our righteous desires with two dramatic parables. The first, known as "The Friend at Midnight," was given to explain "the imperative necessity of earnestness and enduring persistency in praying" (James E. Talmage, *Jesus the Christ,* 25th Ed., S.L.C., Utah: Deseret Book Co., 1956, p. 434).

> And he said unto them, Which of you shall have a friend, and shall go unto him at midnight, and say unto him, Friend, lend me three loaves;
>
> For a friend of mine in his journey is come to me, and I have nothing to set before him?
>
> And he from within shall answer and say, Trouble me not: the door is now shut, and my children are with me in bed; I cannot rise and give thee.
>
> I say unto you, Though he will not rise and give him, because he is his friend, yet because of his importunity he will rise and give him as many as he needeth. (Luke 11:5-8.)

If we were not aware of the infinite goodness of Heavenly Father and of his willingness to grant our worthy requests, we could easily misunderstand the message of this parable. Such a misunderstanding would be especially likely if we were to compare the neighbor's reluctance to help his friend to the way our Father in Heaven responds to our prayers. The intent of the parable was to show the need for persistence, not that we must convince God of the need he already knows we have, nor to persuade him to grant the request. The persistence of our pleading can never increase his already perfect, divine, and infinite generosity, but it can strengthen our faith and increase our desire and worthiness for the granting of the blessing. Consider the inspired interpretation of this parable as given by Apostle James E. Talmage:

> The man to whose home a friend had come at midnight could not let his belated and weary guest go hungry, yet there was no bread in the house. He made his visitor's wants his own, and pleaded at his neighbor's door as though asking for himself. The neighbor was loath to leave his comfortable bed and disturb his household to accommodate another; but, finding that the man at the door was importunate, he at last arose and gave him what he asked, so as to get rid of him and be able to sleep in peace. . .
>
> The hospitable man in the parable had refused to be repulsed; he kept on knocking until the door was opened; and as a result received what he wanted, found what he had set out to obtain. The parable is regarded by some as a difficult one to apply, since it deals with the selfish and comfort-loving element of human nature, and apparently uses this to symbolize God's deliberate delay. The explanation, however, is clear when the context is duly considered. The Lord's lesson was, that if man, with all his selfishness and disinclinations to give, will nevertheless grant what his neighbor with proper purpose asks and continues to ask in spite of objection and temporary refusal, *with assured certainty will God grant what is persistently asked in faith and with righteous intent. No parallelism lies between man's selfish refusal and God's wise and beneficient waiting.* There must be a consciousness of real need for prayer, and real trust in God, to make prayer effective; and *in mercy the Father sometimes delays the granting that the asking may be more fervent. (Jesus the Christ,* pp. 434-435; emphasis added.)

In the second parable Jesus emphasized that we should persist in our prayers until they are granted—or until we are taught the reason for their denial. It is known as "The Importunate Widow." In this case the intent and meaning of the parable was given before it was presented.

> And he spake a parable unto them *to this end, that men ought always to pray, and not to faint;*
>
> Saying, There was in a city a judge, which feared not God, neither regarded man:
>
> And there was a widow in that city; and she came unto him, saying, Avenge me of mine adversary.

> And he would not for a while: but afterward he said within himself, Though I fear not God, nor regard man;
>
> Yet because this widow troubleth me, I will avenge her, lest by her continual coming she weary me.
>
> And the Lord said, Hear what the unjust judge saith. (Luke 18:1-6; see also D&C 101:81-84.)

Here again we could easily misunderstand the meaning if we tried to compare the Lord's response to our prayers to that of the uncaring judge, who finally gave in just to get rid of the widow. Such a comparison would evidence a lack of understanding of the goodness, justice, and impartiality of Heavenly Father. Consider again the inspired words of Apostle Talmage:

> The judge was of wicked character; he denied justice to the widow, who could obtain redress from none other. He was moved to action by the desire to escape the woman's importunity. Let us beware of the error of comparing his selfish action with the ways of God. Jesus did not indicate that as the wicked judge finally yielded to supplication so would God do; but He pointed out that *if even such a being as this judge, who 'feared not God, neither regarded man,' would at last hear and grant the widow's plea, no one should doubt that God, the Just and Merciful, will hear and answer.* (James E. Talmage, *Jesus The Christ,* 25th Ed., S.L.C., Utah: Deseret Book Co., 1956, p. 436; emphasis added.)

All who heed the Lord's admonition to persist in their prayers, not with insistence, but with trust and faith in the Father's will, will be drawn closer to God and will discover more of his love for them. Those who give up on their prayers will not only forfeit the granting of their desires, but even more importantly, will lose the opportunity to grow closer to a Father and a Savior who yearn to be part of their life.

Consider this testimony about the value of persistence from the Book of Mormon.

> And it came to pass that the brother of Jared did cry unto the Lord according to that which had been spoken by the mouth of Jared.
>
> And it came to pass that the Lord did hear the brother of Jared, and had compassion upon him, and said unto him. . .
>
> And there will I bless thee and thy seed, and raise up unto me of thy seed, and of the seed of thy brother, and they who shall go with thee, a great nation. And there shall be none greater than the nation which I will raise up unto me of thy seed, upon all the face of the earth. *And thus I will do unto thee because this long time ye have cried unto me.* (Ether 1:39-40, 43.)

Someone has said that persistence is just another word for faith. When we persist in asking God to grant our desires, we are, in effect, bearing witness to him of our testimony of his goodness and grace. By persistently expressing our desires to him we are manifesting confidence in him. We are saying, in effect, that we know he has the power and the willingness to grant our desires if they are right for us. We are manifesting faith and trust in him when we make claim upon his promises to grant unto us "according to our desires."

On the other hand, consider the lack of faith we manifest if we do not ask him for the things we desire and need by shutting him out, or doubting him so much that we do not even ask. What does it say of our faith when we try to do everything on our own, without asking for his grace and power to assist, to expand, and to purify us?

He Already Knows—So Why Not Pray About It?

Bishop H. Burke Peterson teaches that we should make our prayers a practice in honest expression of our feelings and desires.

> As you feel the need to confide in the Lord or to improve the quality of your visits with him—to pray, if you

> please—may I suggest a process to follow: go where you can be alone, go where you can speak out loud to him. The bedroom, the bathroom, or the closet will do. Now, picture him in your mind's eye. Think to whom you are speaking, control your thoughts—don't let them wander, address him as your Father and your friend. Now *tell him things you really feel* to tell him—not trite phrases that have little meaning, but *have a sincere, heartfelt conversation with him.* Confide in him, thank him, ask him for forgiveness, plead with him, enjoy him, express your love to him, and then listen for his answers. (Melchizedek Priesthood Manual, 1974-75, *When Thou Art Converted, Strengthen Thy Brethren,* p. 117; emphasis added.)

Sometimes we are reluctant to have that honest, open, heartfelt conversation because we are ashamed of our evil, selfish, or unworthy desires. Through the conversion experiences which followed my excommunication, I learned that such feelings do not have to form barriers between me and God, that they could actually draw me closer to him. I learned that he loves me in spite of my faults, and that he does not require or expect me to become perfect all at once. I found that when I was troubled with unworthy desires, I could go to him in prayer and confess them. I could surrender them to him. By telling the Lord that I did not want to feel that way, by telling him that with my conscious will I was rejecting the evil desires, and by asking him to remove them from me, miracles occurred. Through the power of Christ's atonement, he literally blessed me with the grace and strength to overcome such unworthy desires and to cast them from my emotions.

> . . . the Lord will give grace and glory: no good thing will he withhold from them that walk uprightly (Ps. 84:11).

At other times we are reluctant to express our desires to Heavenly Father because of doubts which fill our minds. Doubts such as, "I'm not worthy of such a request. After all I have done, he would never listen to me." Or, "God is much too busy to get involved in such a small matter. I don't dare ask such a thing of God." And, "Who do I think I am to bother God with such a request?"

Everyone has heard the voices of such doubts, voices that crowd out the expression of our desires, voices that hold us back, discourage and break our faith. Some of these doubts come from our own mortality and lack of faith, while others are suggested to our minds by Satan's whisperings. For over thirty years I was hesitant to discuss my desires in prayer for fear of bothering the Lord until he taught me that our prayers never "bother" him. The way we do "bother" him is by refusing to pray, by refusing to present our desires to him.

Because God "comprehendeth all things" (D&C 88:41), and because "all things are naked and opened unto the eyes of him with whom we have to do" (Heb. 4:13), and because "the Lord searcheth all hearts, and understandeth all the imaginations [desires] of the thoughts" (1 Chr. 28:9), it should come as no surprise that God is always aware of our desires, even before we have expressed them to him.

> . . . for your father knoweth what things ye have need of before ye ask him (3 Ne. 13:8; see also Matt. 6:8).

We should be thrilled to know that the God who rules the universe also cares enough to monitor the "thoughts and intents" of our hearts (see D&C 6:16), and that he cares enough about our day-to-day affairs to probe and to know "the secrets of the heart" (see Ps. 44:21).

> Behold and hearken, O ye elders of my church . . . whose prayers I have heard, and whose hearts I know, and whose desires have come up before me (D&C 67:1).

Since God already knows what we feel and desire, and

since we can never hide from him nor surprise him, shouldn't we go ahead and pray in all circumstances, placing our petitions before him, and receiving his counsel and help?

How self-defeating were the ancient Nephites who refused to share their feelings with God, "for they repented not of their iniquities, but did struggle for their lives without calling upon that Being who created them" (Morm. 5:2). How self-defeating we are when we forfeit God's grace by refusing to present our desires to him.

There come times in all our lives when we feel estranged from God and reluctant to pray. But to give in to that Satan-inspired feeling and to "struggle for our lives" without prayer for help will never improve our condition. Trying to hide our feelings from God, who already knows, can never make our situation any better—it only prolongs our undesirable circumstances and makes them worse.

There is no other way to plead for our desires except through prayer. How else can we manifest to him the intensity of our desires? How else can we show him the strength and the direction of our faith and trust? Let us remember that it is not sufficient merely to have faith and trust; it must be expressed. And faith that is expressed is faith that is strengthened. Yet many times we do not need mighty faith so much as we need quiet acceptance. The unquestionable fact is that our Heavenly Father and Savior want to bless us with joy, peace, and success. We do not have to exercise great faith in an established fact, but simply accept it as the truth, and then act in harmony with it. Let us never allow the doubts of mortality to quench our righteous desires and rob us of the confidence we are entitled to by virtue of scriptural promises.

It is encouraging to know that it is not necessary to struggle with the same unworthy desires throughout our entire mortal probation. As we become sanctified and justified before God, he will change our nature and our desires. The converts of Ammon testified of this change. As they surrendered and committed their lives to the Savior, "they did all declare unto the people the selfsame thing—that their hearts had been changed; that they had no more desire to do evil" (Alma 19:33). What God did for them, he is willing to do for us.

No Stones—Unless We Insist

> Or what man is there of you, whom if his son ask bread, will he give him a stone?
>
> Or if he ask a fish, will he give him a serpent?
>
> If ye then, being evil, know how to give good gifts unto your children, *how much more shall your Father which is in heaven give good things to them that ask him?* (Matt. 7:9-11.)

We are promised that Heavenly Father will never give evil or harmful gifts in place of the things for which we ask. This also means that he will never allow a seemingly harmful experience to occur in our lives that he is not prepared to turn to our good (Rom. 8:28). He will never give "stones" when we ask for bread—unless we insist that we want the stones.

We have studied two of the parables which Jesus used to teach the necessity of persistence in prayer. There are, however, some cautions we must observe. Alma, for example, warned that we should "use boldness, but not overbearance" (Alma 38:12). It would be foolish for man to try to force his will upon the Father by overbearing prayers, because it is possible to persist in prayer with such arrogant insistence and lack of submission that God will go ahead and grant our "stones." Sometimes we are so stubborn that the only way we can learn that God knows best is to suffer the harmful consequences of our childish demands. Overly insistent prayers, prayers of demand instead of request, can lead us into some very painful learning experiences, as explained by Apostle Ezra Taft Benson.

> Sometimes He temporarily grants to men their unwise requests in order that they might learn from their own sad experiences. Some refer to this as the 'Samuel principle.' The children of Israel wanted a king like all the other nations. The prophet Samuel was displeased and prayed to the Lord about it. The Lord responded by saying, "Samuel, they have not rejected thee, but they have rejected me, that I should not reign over them." The Lord told Samuel to warn the people of the consequences if they had a king. Samuel gave them the warning. But they still insisted on their king. So God gave them a king and let them suffer. They learned the hard way. God wanted it to be otherwise, *but within certain bounds he grants unto men according to their desires.* Bad experiences are an expensive school that only fools keep going to. See 1 Sam. 8. (Jesus Christ—Gifts and Expectations, *The New Era,* May 1975, p. 17; emphasis added. See also Alma 29:4-5.)

A proper expression of our desires will always include our permission, indeed, our request, that God would withhold, or modify, the granting of our desires if his superior will and foreknowledge indicate that what we ask would be harmful or inappropriate. In this way we are asking God to protect us from our own ignorance. While Heavenly Father has given us our agency and promised to strictly honor our choices, he has also been careful to warn that insisting upon inappropriate desires "shall turn unto your condemnation" (D&C 88:64-65).

In conclusion, then, these warnings do not mean we should reduce the fervor or persistence of our prayers. Never! What they do mean is that we should always recognize the superiority of God's wisdom and foreknowledge of the consequences of our desires, and that "one of the things we should most often pray for is to know what we should most often pray for" (*Conference Report,* October 1960, p. 90).

VIII

Promises

God Never Changes

There are three ways to know God. (1) Through the scriptural accounts of how he has dealt with man in the past. (2) Through the testimonies of others of how he has dealt with them. (3) Through our own experiences as he relates to us.

One requirement for trust in God's promises is the knowledge, or faith, that the Father and the Son never change their characteristics in their dealings with mankind. James tells us that "a double minded man is unstable in all his ways" (James 1:8). Because God is perfectly stable, perfectly constant and consistent, and most importantly, perfectly predictable, we have every right to expect him to respond to us just as he has responded to others in the past.

The scriptures are replete with the assurance of God's constancy. "From eternity to eternity he is the same. . ." (D&C 76:4). "Jesus Christ [is] the same yesterday, and today, and forever" (Heb. 13:8). ". . . the Father of lights, with whom is no variableness, neither shadow of turning" (James 1:17). "For do we not read that God is the same yesterday, today, and forever, and in him there is no variableness neither shadow of changing?" (Morm. 9:9). Without the assurance that we can depend upon the constancy of God's words and feelings, the constancy of his attitude, love, and goodwill, his patience and forgiveness, without the assurance that all his other attributes will remain the same, how could we ever dare to trust him or place our faith and hope in his promises?

God Never Lies

Our Heavenly Father and Savior are Gods of truth. They cannot lie. They cannot, will not, and do not change or deny their promises. Therefore, we can have total faith and confidence in every promise we find in the scriptures.

> . . . the idea that he is a God of truth and cannot lie, is equally as necessary to the exercise of faith in him as the idea of his unchangeableness. For without the idea that he was a God of truth and could not lie, the confidence necessary to be placed in his word in order to the exercise of faith in him could not exist. But having the idea that he is not [like] man, that he cannot lie, it gives power to the minds of men to exercise faith in him. (Joseph Smith, *Lectures on Faith,* 3:22, comp. N.B. Lundwall, P.O. Box 2033, S.L.C., Utah, p. 36.)

Scriptures on which we can base this confidence are plentiful, for God has repeated the assurance many times. For example, "If we believe not, yet he abideth faithful: *he cannot deny himself*" (2 Tim. 2:13). ". . . I cannot deny my word" (D&C 39:16). ". . . it is impossible for him to deny his word" (Alma 11:34). "I, the Lord, promise the faithful and cannot lie" (D&C 62:6). ". . . and my word shall be verified at this time as it hath hitherto been verified" (D&C 5:20). "And whosoever shall believe in my name, doubting nothing, *unto him will I confirm all my words,* even unto the ends of the earth" (Morm. 9:25).

As promised in the last verse, not only can we place unqualified trust upon all that we read in God's word, but we may expect to have his promises "confirmed" both by personal revelation and by having them fulfilled in our own experiences.

God Is Impartial

Our Heavenly Father and Savior treat everyone equally, without partiality or respect of persons. "For there is no respect of persons with God" (Rom. 2:11). "For there is no difference between the Jew and the Greek: For the same Lord over all is rich unto all that call upon him" (Rom. 10:12). ". . . and he inviteth them all to come unto him and partake of his goodness; and he denieth none that come unto him, black and white, bond and free, male and female; and he remembereth the heathen; and all are alike unto God, both Jew and Gentile" (2 Ne. 26:33).

> But it is also necessary that men should have an idea that he is no respecter of persons, for with the idea of all other excellencies in his character, and this one wanting, men could not exercise faith in him; *because if he were a respecter of persons, they could not tell what their privileges were,* nor how far they were authorized to exercise faith in him, or whether they were authorized to do it at all, but all must be confusion (Joseph Smith, *Lectures on Faith,* 3:23, comp. N.B. Lundwall, P.O. Box 2033, S.L.C., Utah, p. 36; emphasis added).

When the Lord places the record of his dealings with specific individuals or groups of people in the scriptures, he does it to show that we have the right and privilege to lay claim on any principle of promise that we find recorded there. "And now I give unto you a commandment that what I say unto one I say unto all . . ." (D&C 61:18). "And now, verily I say unto you, and what I say unto one I say unto all. . ." (D&C 61:36). "Therefore, what I say unto one I say unto all. . ." (D&C 82:5).

What God, who never changes, has done for others, he will do for us when we are willing to qualify.

An Absolute Guarantee

Everything God promises will be fulfilled exactly as he says without the slightest variation. "Who am I, saith the Lord, that have promised and have not fulfilled?" (D&C 58:31). "For I will fulfill my promises which I have made unto the children of men. . ." (2 Ne. 10:17). ". . . and as the words have gone forth out of my mouth even so shall they be fulfilled. . ." (D&C 29:30). "What I the Lord have spoken, I have spoken, and I excuse not myself; and though the heavens and the earth pass away, my word shall not pass away, but shall all be fulfilled. . ." (D&C 1:38).

Why has God repeated this message so often? Because he knows how easy it is to doubt, and because he wants us to trust him and to rely on his promises. "For as I, the Lord God, liveth, even so my words cannot return void, for as they go forth out of my mouth they must be fulfilled" (Moses 4:30). ". . . I have spoken it, I will also bring it to pass; I have purposed it, I will also do it" (Isa. 46:11). ". . . he fulfilleth the words which he hath given, and he lieth not, but fulfilleth all his words" (3 Ne. 27:18).

> All I can do is take him at his word . . . he did not say anything that he did not mean. He made no promise that he is not prepared to keep (N. Eldon Tanner, *Outstanding Stories by General Authorities,* comp. Leon R. Hartshorn, S.L.C., Utah: Deseret Book Co., 1970, p. 209).

The One Power That Can Prevent God's Promises

> . . . What power shall stay the heavens? As well might man stretch forth his puny arm to stop the Missouri River in its decreed course, or to turn it upstream, as to hinder the Almighty from pouring down knowledge [and blessings] from heaven upon the heads of the Latter-day Saints. (D&C 121:33.)

There is only one power strong enough to prevent God

from blessing us in fulfillment of his promises. It is not the power of Lucifer and all of his demons, for no evil spirit can thwart God's power. Only one person has the power to withhold God's blessings. Ourself! Only by failing to fulfill the requirements associated with God's blessings can we prevent his mercy and grace from flowing into our lives. Whenever we feel abandoned, or feel that we are outside of God's grace, the fault never rests with him. Sooner or later we must all come to the realization that when things are not right in our lives, we must stop shaking our fists at the heavens and learn to look inside our own hearts for the cause.

> I command and men obey not; I revoke and they receive not the blessing.
>
> Then they say in their hearts: This is not the work of the Lord, for his promises are not fulfilled. But wo unto such, for their reward lurketh beneath, and not from above. (D&C 58:32-33.)
>
> For all who will have a blessing at my hands shall abide the law which was appointed for that blessing, and the conditions thereof, as were instituted from before the foundation of the world (D&C 132:5; see also D&C 130:20-21).
>
> I, the Lord, am bound when ye do what I say; but when ye do not what I say, ye have no promise (D&C 82:10).

These scriptures make it clear that the responsibility for the flow of blessings from heaven rests upon us and not upon God. He has established the laws and conditions that govern our lives and made them plain to our understanding. We are told that "all truth is independent in that sphere in which God has placed it, to act for itself . . ." (D&C 93:30). Hence, if we qualify, the blessings will flow. If we disobey, our violation of the law restrains God's ability to bless us. The God who issued the following warning cannot deny his word.

> For behold, the Lord hath said: I will not succor my people in the day of their transgression; but I will hedge up their ways that they prosper not; and their doings shall be as a stumbling block before them (Mosiah 7:29).
>
> Yea, they turned back and tempted God, and limited the Holy One of Israel (Ps. 78:41).

On one occasion, as I was walking down a hallway where I work, I had this truth made plain to me. On this particular occasion it was necessary for me to walk very slowly because of the crippled, twisted and distorted body of a custodian, who slowly stumbled along ahead of me. I had often felt sorrow and pity for this man, but on this occasion my heart was really drawn to him. As I looked at my strong, healthy hands I thought, "Oh, that I had the power of my Savior who healed so many people. If only I could reach out as he did, and take this crippled brother in my arms and bless him to health as I know Jesus would want to do if he were here."

I am grateful for that experience, for it brought me closer to the Savior in two ways. First, I think I felt in some small measure the joy that Jesus must have felt as the people thronged to him for a touch, or a word of blessing. For the first time I glimpsed what it would be like for him who healed so many, and that was a precious experience.

Secondly, I grew closer to him through the realization that even if I had the Lord's power, the choice to heal this man would not be mine to give, but would depend upon the agency and the faith of the crippled one. Tears came as I felt the utter sorrow and frustration that Jesus must have felt, and still feels today, as he reaches out to touch our lives with his power—only to have us shun him through doubt, wickedness, or indifference.

I urge the reader to imagine the sorrow the Lord must feel, having these mighty powers and blessings that he desires to share with us, but cannot because of our doubt and indifference. It is a moving discovery.

IX
Pride

Why do we include a chapter on pride in a study of the Lord's grace and power? Because pride is offensive to God and is devastating to our spiritual progress. Any form of pride forms a barrier that restricts or prevents the flow of his grace into our life. Wouldn't it be tragic to spend years struggling to improve ourselves, years of trying to be more worthy before our God, years of trying to grow closer to him, and all the time carry within us an undetected vanity which prevented the very goal we seek?

What kind of pride could go undetected by an active Latter-day Saint? Pride is usually thought of in terms of vanity, conceit, haughtiness and arrogance. In other words, it is pretending to ourselves (and others) to be more, or better, than we really are. It is trying to deceive God by showing only our "good side." This type of pride rarely goes undetected when we are honest with ourselves. However, it is quite possible that even when we are free of these obvious elements of pride we may still fall victim to other, more subtle forms of pride which are, perhaps, even more devastating. Why? Because they so often masquerade under the applaudable guise of self-reliance.

In the Psalms David asked the important question, "Who shall ascend into the hill of the Lord? or who shall stand in his holy place?" (Ps. 24:3.) His answer listed three qualifications: virtue of act and thought, truthfulness, and the absence of pride. He said: "He that hath clean hands, and a pure heart; who hath not lifted up his soul unto vanity, nor sworn deceitfully" (Ps 24:4).

What does it mean to "lift up our souls" in pride and vanity? One of the greatest dangers of pride is an over-confidence in the power of our own abilities. To have self-respect and self-esteem, however, is of vital importance in achieving success in life and in our stewardships in God's kingdom. The Lord wants us to have feelings of self-worth and self-confidence. Nevertheless, in the following verse we are warned of the danger of having our self-confidence and self-esteem "lifted up beyond that which is good." That is to say, to the point where we lose our realization of the dependence we have, and should feel, upon Jesus Christ.

> Yea, wo shall come unto you because of that pride which ye have suffered to enter your hearts, *which has lifted you up beyond that which is good*. . . (Hel. 7:26).

The following definitions of pride, derived from scriptural descriptions, can help us discover the deceptions of Satan which so often mislead us into a dependence upon ourselves which goes "beyond that which is good."

1. Pride can be as simple as a feeling that we are living a good enough life, and do not need any major improvements.

2. Pride can also be an admission that we do need some improvements, but that we are perfectly capable of making the necessary changes without divine help. ("I'll do it myself!")

3. Pride is having such strong feelings of shame for our weaknesses or sins that we are not willing to discuss them openly and honestly with our Heavenly Father or his priesthood representatives.

4. Perhaps the most subtle and dangerous form of

pride is the well-intended, but over-insistent determination to make ourselves good enough for God all by ourselves. That is, by relying upon our own strengths and will power alone, instead of humbly allowing God to be a part of our growth and improvement.

5. Pride is any form of resistance to divine assistance.

How Does God Feel About Pride?

The scriptures contain over one hundred and fifty statements about the dangers of man's pride. Many of them warn us that God's feeling toward this spiritual cancer is one of actual hatred! (Speaking, of course, of the attitude, not the person.)

> These six things doth the Lord hate: yea, seven are an abomination unto him: A proud look . . . (Prov. 6:16-17).

> Every one that is proud in heart is an abomination to the Lord. . . he shall not be unpunished (Prov. 16:5).

It is important to know what God does, and what he is going to do in our lives about unrepented pride. He knows that most of our mistakes and transgressions are the simple result of mortality, and he is extremely patient with such faults as long as we are sincerely trying to overcome them. But pride, he has warned, he will not tolerate!

> . . . him that hath an high look and a proud heart will not I suffer (Ps. 101:5).

> God resisteth the proud, but giveth grace unto the humble (James 4:6; see also 1 Pet. 5:5).

Why is this language so extreme? Because "The wicked, through the pride of his countenance, will not seek after God: God is not in all his thoughts" (Ps. 10:4). These alarming warnings should cause us to reflect seriously upon our lives, but there are other warnings we must also consider. The most often repeated is, "And whosoever shall exalt himself shall be abased. . ." (Matt. 23:12; see also 2 Ne. 12:17; 23:12; Hel. 11:37). These scriptures do not threaten us with a vindictive punishment. Rather, they express the love of a patient and tender Father who seeks, through every means available, to bring circumstances into our lives which will teach us how much we need him. But until we learn to humble ourselves before him, we have the terrifying warning that, not only will he refuse to tolerate our deliberate vanity, he will actually withdraw himself far from us until such time as we are willing to renew a relationship on his terms.

> Though the Lord be high, yet hath he respect unto the lowly: *but the proud he knoweth afar off* (Ps. 138:6).
>
> . . . when we undertake . . . to gratify our pride, our vain ambition . . . behold, *the heavens withdraw themselves;* the Spirit of the Lord is grieved. . . (D&C 121:37).

How awful it would be to pray for help to a God who felt so "grieved" over our pride that he felt it necessary to "resist" and "withdraw" from us. Perhaps we have already experienced this dilemma without realizing the reason that our prayers were so difficult and ineffective.

There is nothing we can do to alter God's stubborn love for us. Nevertheless, our pride grieves him sorely, for he knows only too well the pain and delays which it brings into our lives. So, in spite of his sorrow to leave us, he still must withdraw. God will never impose himself upon us against our will. Regretfully and painfully he withdraws from our stubborn pride, leaving us to learn the lessons of life the hard way, while he watches hopefully "from afar off" for us to learn how much we need him.

God, Man And Amoebas

One of the major origins of man's pride is the overconfidence which so often results from man's acquisition of knowledge. How easy it is to persuade ourselves that we know better than God.

> O the vainness, and the frailties, and the foolishness of men! When they are learned they think they are wise, and they hearken not unto the counsels of God, for they set it aside, supposing they know of themselves, *wherefore their wisdom is foolishness and it profiteth them not.* And they shall perish. (2 Ne. 9:28.)

When a person is separated from the Spirit of the Lord by sin, there are many ways for the Lord to reach into his life and move him toward repentance. But when a person is self-satisfied in his own knowledge, it is extremely difficult for the Lord to influence him because there is no room left for the promptings of the Spirit. Thus, he denies himself of growth, unity with God, and grace.

So great is the danger of being overly independent because of our knowledge that God has warned repeatedly to beware, for "knowledge puffeth up. . ." (1 Cor. 8:1). "Be not wise in thine own eyes. . ." (Prov. 3:7). "Wo unto them that are wise in their own eyes, and prudent in their own sight!" (Isa. 5:21). "Seest thou a man wise in his own conceit? There is more hope of a fool than of him" (Prov. 26:12).

> . . . the wise, and the learned, . . . who are puffed up because of their learning, and their wisdom . . . they are they whom he despiseth; and *save they shall cast these things away, and consider themselves fools before God, and come down in the depths of humility, he will not open unto them* (2 Ne. 9:42).

On the other hand, we are told that "the glory of God is intelligence" (D&C 93:36), and that "the Lord is a God of knowledge" (1 Sam. 2:3). We are also told that man must emulate this trait of godly knowledge for "it is impossible for a man to be saved in ignorance" (D&C 131:6), and that "my people are destroyed for lack of knowledge" (Hosea 4:6). In the day of judgment "a man shall be commended according to his wisdom" (Prov. 12:8). "A man is saved no faster than he gets knowledge" (Teachings of the Prophet Joseph Smith, 7th Ed., comp. Joseph Fielding Smith, S.L.C., Utah: Deseret Book Co., 1951, p. 217).

Now let us consider for a moment. On one hand the prophets stress the importance of gaining knowledge and understanding. But on the other hand they seem to criticize the value of man's knowledge. How is this seeming contradiction resolved? The truth is that there is no scriptural conflict. The conflict exists in man, not in the scriptures. The scriptures are simply a warning against the tendency in man's carnal nature to become self-sufficient and self-satisfied because of his knowledge. The Lord is simply warning us against that part of our "natural man" which tends to get "puffed up" and lose humility. When we lose humility and try to walk in the light of our own knowledge instead of in the light of Christ, we shut him out and forfeit the grace that he is so anxious to share with us.

The 1969-70 Gospel Doctrine Manual quotes 3 Ne. 12:3 thus: "Blessed are the poor in spirit who come unto me, for theirs is the kingdom of heaven," and then makes the following comments:

> By the poor in spirit Jesus did not mean those who are utterly without spirituality. Many people's lives are choked with pride. They are arrogant. They are a law unto themselves. Like wild stallions they bow to no higher authority. They are self-sufficient. *Unless they change and come to the Lord with a broken heart and a contrite spirit, they are unable to make spiritual progress.* The acknowledgement of God as a higher authority and the subjugation of oneself in a humble, prayerful, and sweet

> attitude is the first step one must take to prepare himself for spiritual growth. (*In His Footsteps Today,* S.L.C., Utah: Deseret Sunday School Union, 1969, p. 286; emphasis added.)

The Lord feels that it is crucial for us to recognize the tremendous difference between his mind and ours, and he has tried to show us the contrast on many occasions such as that in the following description:

> For my thoughts are not your thoughts, neither are your ways my ways, saith the Lord.
>
> *For as the heavens are higher than the earth,* so are my ways higher than your ways, and my thoughts than your thoughts. (Isa. 55:8-9.)

How high are the heavens above us? The nearest star is millions of light years away, and this is the Lord's contrast between his mind and ours! If we could even begin to comprehend the vast gulf which exists between our puny, finite understanding and the infinite wisdom of our Heavenly Father and Savior who "know all things," we would stand, no, we would kneel in humble awe. I suspect that someday we will discover that the gulf between their intelligence and ours is even greater than the gulf which separates our intelligence and abilities from that of the lowly amoeba. Where is room for pride?

A Broken Heart And A Contrite Spirit

The most treacherous form of pride comes from overconfidence in our own self-sufficiency, knowledge and abilities. None of us are immune to the dangers of pride. It is part of the traits of our "natural man." As Helaman warned, "Yea, how quick [are the children of men] to be lifted up in pride; yea, how quick to boast . . ." (Hel. 12:5).

We have been warned repeatedly that any form of pride

will make us vulnerable to the temptations and influence of Satan. "But beware of pride, lest thou shouldst enter into temptation" (D&C 23:1). ". . . lest being lifted up with pride he fall into the condemnation of the devil" (1 Tim. 3:6).

> Be not ashamed, neither confounded; but be admonished in all your high-mindedness and pride, *for it bringeth a snare upon your souls* (D&C 90:17).

We have learned that pride leads us away from God, away from peace, away from love and growth and from all that is good. And where does it lead? "Nevertheless, thou hast seen great sorrow, for thou hast rejected me many times because of pride and the cares of the world" (D&C 39:9).

What an offense it must be to God when he has promised to help and guide us and bring us wisdom and strength from our experiences—only to have us turn our backs and, in effect, say to him, "Don't bother with this, Lord, I'll handle it myself." On the other hand, the true confidence, the true strength we should seek is that which was expressed so beautifully by Ammon:

> Yea, I know that I am nothing; as to my strength I am weak; therefore I will not boast of myself, but I will boast of my God, for in his strength I can do all things. . . (Alma 26:12; see also Philip. 4:13).

There is no use pretending when we approach God. Like it or not, he knows us better than we know ourselves. Therefore, we must break ourselves; yes, break our very hearts, by coming to him just as we are, fully acknowledging to him and to ourselves our weaknesses, our faults, sins, bad habits, indeed, our entire unworthiness and need for him. Nothing will do but a full admission of how much we need him. And the amazing and joyful truth is that when we do come to him honestly and openly, he will respond to us so much faster than he can when we come attempting to hold our faults behind our backs as if he didn't know about them.

As we suffer the pain of this experience, we can also receive the miracle referred to in the scriptures as "a broken heart and a contrite spirit." This, we will discover, is but another way of hearing our Heavenly Father saying, "Welcome home, my child."

X

Submission

Agency And Choice

In the Garden of Eden God gave mankind the power of his own agency (see Moses 7:32). As man uses this agency to make decisions and choose alternatives, there are four powers or types of will upon which he may base his choices: (1) The will of God; (2) The will of man; (3) The carnal will of man's flesh; and (4) The will of Satan. Every choice made by man ascribes loyalty to one of these four authorities.

In the Garden of Eden man made a temporary choice to follow Satan's will by partaking of the forbidden fruit. This act of disobedience caused man to "become subject" to his own will.

> And now, ye see by this that our first parents were cut off both temporally and spiritually from the presence of the Lord; and thus we see *they became subjects to follow after their own will* (Alma 42:7).

Even worse than falling subject to his own inexperienced will is the terrifying fact that fallen man has also become subject to the "will of the devil."

> . . . Adam . . . partook of the forbidden fruit and transgressed the commandment, wherein *he became subject to the will of the devil, because he yielded unto temptation* (D&C 29:40).

It is the will of Satan to prevent our victory, and to so enslave us that we become permanently subject to his will, being miserable forever as he is. Each time we yield to temptation we deliberately choose to subject ourselves even more to "the will of the devil." What a tragic way to use our will!

> Know ye not, that to whom ye yield yourselves servants to obey, his servants ye are to whom ye obey; whether of sin unto death, or of obedience unto righteousness? (Rom. 6:16).

The next two verses present the alarming fact that our mortal flesh also has a will of its own, which, as part of "the natural man," is aligned with the will of the devil, and is in opposition to the will of God.

> Wherefore, my beloved brethren, reconcile yourselves to the will of God, and not to the will of the devil and the [will of the] flesh. . . (2 Ne. 10:24).

> Let not sin therefore reign in your mortal body, that ye should obey it in the lusts thereof (Rom. 6:12; see also Rom. 7:23-24).

Anyone who has seriously attempted to alter their physical habits (such as overeating, temper, exercise, lust, etc.) has encountered the strength of this "will of the flesh." Obedience and subjection to "the will of the flesh" will guarantee our damnation. (See Rom. 8:4-8.) Perhaps the most sobering of all the revelations regarding the significance of fallen and mortal man becoming subject unto his own will, to the will of his flesh, or to the will of the devil, is the fact that God is going to allot to each person the rewards or punishments which are in strict accordance with the use he made of his will.

> . . . Yea, I know that *he alloteth unto men according to their wills,* whether they be unto salvation or unto destruction (Alma 29:4).

In order for man to live a Christlike life, he must learn to conquer and subdue the "will of his flesh" so that it becomes entirely obedient to the rule of his spirit. He must also resist the "will of Satan" until the devil loses all power and influence over his choices. But even this is not enough. Each person is also required to surrender the power of his own personal will to the care and keeping of God's infinitely superior will. The scriptures refer to this good judgment as the act of "submission," or "yielding" of our agency to the will of God.

In comparison to God's knowledge, man's mortal will is ignorant and inexperienced. It is inferior to God's perfect will and is often contrary to man's best good, because of his preoccupation with the values and priorities of this temporary world. The "natural man's" view is shortsighted and seeks comfort over perfection. Following the worldly and natural inclinations of his own will, or the will of his flesh, in preference to God's will, places man in such a condition of opposition to God that he is actually called his enemy. (See Mosiah 3:19.)

It is God's will to help us achieve victory over everything that prevents us from being like him. His holy and perfect will is based upon the eternal perspectives that will exalt man and help him to obtain the perfection and fulness of joy which is possessed by those celestial beings who have already proven themselves victorious. How foolish the natural man is for choosing the temporary over the eternal!

It is only when we use our will to seek his will, and then "surrender," "submit," "yield," or "reconcile" ourselves to God's will (in preference to our own) that we place ourselves in a position to receive his grace in our endeavors. Only through willing submission to him can we gain true freedom and victory over all circumstances of life.

The prophet Ether exemplified the truly submissive attitude which no longer fights against the lessons of mortality, but says, in effect, "It no longer matters what happens to me, as long as my heart is right with God."

> Whether the Lord will that I be translated, or that I suffer the will of the Lord in the flesh, *it mattereth not, if it so be that I am saved in the kingdom of God* (Ether 15:34).

As we discovered in the last chapter, choosing one's own will in preference to the will of God is the height of vanity and foolishness. Man is so inferior to God that we should be overwhelmed with gratitude for his condescension in teaching us the better way of life.

> . . . I give unto you directions how you may act before me, that it may turn to you for your salvation (D&C 82:9).

> Wherefore be ye not unwise, but understanding what the will of the Lord is (Eph. 5:17).

The Two Wills Of God

> Hearken, O ye elders of my church, and give ear to my word, and learn of me what I will concerning you . . . (D&C 58:1).

God's will for mankind has two categories. First is that part of his will which pertains equally to all men, and which we usually think of as the moral and ethical principles, or "the commandments." Secondly is that part of his will which is personal and is tailored to the individual. Examples of this second part of his will would be found in Church callings and in answers to individual prayers. Jesus demonstrated this dual nature of God's will for man when he warned the Prophet Joseph Smith that if the Saints expected to receive an inheritance in the celestial kingdom, they must "prepare themselves" by obedience to both parts of his will. He said we must not only obey the commandments, but that we must also learn to recognize and obey his will for us individually.

> Verily, thus saith the Lord: It shall come to pass that every soul who forsaketh his sins and cometh unto me, and

> calleth on my name, *and obeyeth my voice, and keepeth my commandments,* shall see my face and know that I am (D&C 93:1).

If his "voice" were the same as his commandments, the Lord would not have repeated himself. There is no commandment that says an individual must serve as a bishop or stake president, as a Relief Society or Primary worker, or any other position in order to obtain the celestial kingdom. But if the Lord issues such a call to an individual through priesthood channels, he is then placing that "requirement" upon the person.

> For if you will that I give unto you a place in the celestial world, you must prepare yourselves by doing the things which I have *commanded* you [his universal will for all men] and *required* of you [his will for us as individuals] (D&C 78:7).

By issuing such calls, the Lord is manifesting part of his individual will to that specific person, and should he then refuse the call (or accept it but treat it casually), he would be failing to "prepare" himself for celestial glory by neglecting something which God has "required" of him.

It was not a "commandment" to serve as a pioneer, but such a sacrifice was "required" of many of our forefathers. Those who obeyed were thereby prepared for a glory they could never have obtained by rejecting the call and remaining behind in comfort. The Lord loves each of us enough to provide personally designed opportunities for our individual service and sacrifice which will, for us, become "requirements."

As we partake of the sacrament each Sunday, we are convenanting (if we mean what we are doing) with our Heavenly Father to remember the Lord Jesus Christ at all times during the coming week. Heavenly Father, in turn, promises to reward this spiritual concentration with the endowment of the Spirit of Jesus Christ to be with us at all times. Why is this ordinance so vital that it is repeated every seven days? Because being attended by the Spirit of Jesus Christ not only helps us feel and live more holy, but it also teaches us his personal will for our daily walk.

> For by my Spirit will I enlighten them, and by my power will I make known unto them the secrets of my will. . . (D&C 76:10).
>
> . . . feast upon the words of Christ; for behold, *the words of Christ will tell you all things what ye should do* (2 Ne. 32:3).
>
> For it shall be given you by the Holy Ghost to know my will. . . (D&C 124:5).

The Meaning Of Submission

The commandment to "yield" and "submit" ourselves to the two wills of God, to place ourselves totally in the hands of the Lord, is presented repeatedly throughout scripture.

> And now I would that ye should be humble, and be submissive and gentle; easy to be entreated; full of patience and long-suffering . . . (Alma 7:23).
>
> Now be ye not stiffnecked, as your fathers were, but yield yourselves unto the Lord . . . and serve the Lord your God, that the fierceness of his wrath may turn away from you (2 Chr. 30:8).
>
> God resisteth the proud, but giveth grace unto the humble.
>
> Submit yourselves therefore to God (James 4:6-7).

Each of us must choose between two alternatives. Either we yield our heart and will to God, or we hold back, trying to make our own way with hearts that are self-willed and resistant to his supposed intrusions. Learning to submit ourselves into his keeping is a wonderfully exciting experience in spiritual growth, but it goes far beyond obedience, or mere compliance with the "letter of the law."

The Lord is looking for a people "who know their hearts are honest, and are broken, and their spirits contrite, and are willing to observe their covenants by sacrifice—yea, every sacrifice which I, the Lord, shall command—they are accepted of me" (D&C 97:8; see also D&C 136:31). Submission means we are willing to bear our personal "crosses" (requirements) no matter how great the pain, no matter how heavy the load, and no matter how hard or long the labor. It not only means a willingness, but also a desire to place our hearts and wills, our entire selves, upon the altar of sacrifice without knowing or even caring what the Lord will require of us. For "Behold, the Lord requireth the heart and a willing mind" (D&C 64:34). How can we dare to do such a thing? Because of our faith and trust that God will never require anything that is harmful or anything that we, with his help, cannot do. And also because we know that when we surrender to the Lord all that we are and have, he, in turn, commits to us all that he is and all that he can do, so that eventually, through his great power and grace, we will inherit with him all that there is in celestial perfection and glory. (See D&C 84:38.)

Submitting our lives to God's will does not mean that he expects us to become like robots, obeying mechanically without thought.

> Some people say, "Lord, help my will to crumble." God doesn't want a broken down will that He can dominate. He wants your will whole and in submission to His will, so that the two of you can work together in unity (Kenneth Copeland, *The Laws of Prosperity,* Fort Worth, Texas: Kenneth Copeland Publications, 1974, p. 15).

Submission is a joyful willingness, it is like "jumping at the chance" to place ourselves in total harmony with God, not because it was commanded, but because we know that it is better for us. Perhaps an example will help.

Through long years of sacrifice and saving we have finally been able to purchase our dream car. Automotive perfection worth over two years of our salary. It has everything we have always wanted. Its design, its color, the interior, the engine, everything is complete and perfect. But everytime we drive or park it we are concerned with its protection and maintenance. What if it gets dented or scratched? What will we do when it requires maintenance or repairs? We love the car, but we know that we are not qualified to care for it as it deserves.

Then we remember that our brother is a master mechanic with a lifetime of experience in automotive maintenance. "Bring your car to me," he says, "and I will maintain it for you as if it were my own." Willingly, indeed joyfully, we "surrender" (yield or submit) the upkeep and maintenance to him. Why? How can we dare to let go of the control of our priceless treasure? It is not because we no longer care, but because of how much we do care! It is because we know that he can care for it so much better than we can. We are thrilled to yield control to his superior knowledge and experience because we are aware of our own inferiority and because we want only the best.

And so it is with the surrendering of our lives into the care and keeping of our Master, Jesus Christ. It is a wonderful experience to know that the Lord, the Master, is in charge of our life and that we can trust him at all times to guide us toward that which is best for us. We all come to him with dents and scratches, but it does not matter to the Savior so much what our past has been, once we give him full charge of our present and future. The Lord is perfectly willing to take our unworthy hand as long as it is offered to him with a submissive and repentant attitude.

The two poems that follow provide a striking comparison between the aspirations of the "natural man" to set himself supreme and self-sufficient, and the humble recognition of a disciple's dependence upon his Savior. They are taken from a comparison in the 1974-75 Melchizedek Priesthood Manual, pp. 81-82. "The first poem," says the manual, "expresses exaggerated self-sufficiency." The second poem was written by Apostle Orson Whitney as an answer to the first.

INVICTUS

Out of the night that covers me,
Black as the pit from pole to pole,
I thank whatever Gods may be
For my unconquerable soul.

In the fall clutch of circumstance
I have not winced nor cried aloud.
Under bludgeonings of chance
My head is bloody, but unbowed.

Beyond this place of wrath and tears
Looms but the horrors of the shade.
And yet the menace of the years
Finds, and shall find me, unafraid.

It matters not how straight the gate,
How charged with punishment the scroll.
I am the master of my fate;
I am the captain of my soul.

— William Ernest Henley

THE SOUL'S CAPTAIN

Art thou in truth? Then what of him
Who bought thee with his blood?
Who plunged into devouring seas
And snatched thee from the flood?

And bore for all our fallen race
What none but him could bear—
The God who died that man might live,
And endless glory share?

Of what avail thy vaunted strength,
Apart from his vast might?
Pray that his light may pierce the glow
That thou mayest see aright.

Men are as bubbles on the wave,
As leaves upon the tree.
Thou, captain of thy soul, forsooth!
Who gave the place to thee?

Free will is thine—free agency
To wield for right or wrong;
But thou must answer unto Him
To whom all souls belong.

Bend to the dust that "unbowed head,"
Small part of life's great whole!
And see in him, and him alone,
The captain of thy soul.

—*Orson F. Whitney*

Following the two poems, the manual asks the following two soul-searching questions. The answers we find within our own heart will be important factors in our ability to call down grace from the heavens.

1. "Do you feel that you depend upon the Savior for spiritual and temporal well-being?"

2. "Or do you suppose that your own genius and strength are sufficient to guarantee your day-to-day success?"

Your objective is to seek to comprehend the influence of Christ's power in your life, that without him you can do nothing (John 15:5), in order that you may work out your salvation with increased humility and with a greater sense of trust and dependence upon him (*When Thou Art Converted, Strengthen Thy Brethren,* pp. 81-82).

Brigham Young said that we must so live as "to be sanctified, that every thought and desire and feeling may be brought into subjection to the will of God" (*Journal of Discourses,* Vol. 11, p. 289). God's will for us is already perfect. We cannot add, take away, or change one iota of his will and improve it. He always knows what is best, and he wants us to know this so that we will respond to him reverently, obediently, and submissively.

> Cause me to know the way wherein I should walk; for I lift up my soul unto thee (Ps. 143:8).

"Not My Will But Thine Be Done"

The Lord has used many compelling examples to illustrate the depth of dependence which he wants us to enjoy in our submissive obedience. We will now review six of these examples.

1. *The relationship of a tool to its craftsman*

> Shall the axe boast itself against him that heweth therewith? or shall the saw magnify itself against him that shaketh it? (Isa. 10:15).
>
> . . . shall the work say of him that made it, He made me not? or shall the thing framed say of him that framed it, He had no understanding? (Isa. 29:16).

Isaiah used the example of tools because it is obvious that no matter how perfect the tool is, it can never, by itself, accomplish any good. It must be placed in the hands of a skilled craftsman. Of course, Isaiah was not really talking about axes and saws. He was talking about our relationship to God. Are we willing to set aside our pride and acknowledge that with God holding us in his hand and guiding us in life's experiences, we will always be superior to that which we could achieve without him? Must we go through life insisting on becoming a "self-made" man, or can we be wise enough to surrender our making to the Master Craftsman?

> Know ye that the Lord he is God: it is he that hath made us, and not we ourselves . . . (Ps. 100:3).

2. *The relationship of clay to its potter*

> But now, O Lord, thou art our Father; we are the clay, and thou our potter; and we are all the work of thy hand (Isa. 64:8).

> Wo unto him that striveth with his maker! . . . Shall the clay say to him that fashioneth it, What makest thou? (Isa. 45:9; see also Rom. 9:20-21.)

God compared to a potter? Man compared to a lump of clay? What a strange analogy this would be if we did not understand that Isaiah was only teaching us how much we need the Lord in our daily life. "Behold, as the clay is in the potter's hand, so are ye in mine hand, O house of Israel" (Jer. 18:6).

When we judge ourselves in terms of a finished vessel, we feel inferior and unworthy because we know that we are far from perfection. But when we see ourselves as unfinished clay in the hands of the Master Potter, we have the confident assurance that he will make of us a far more beautiful vessel than we could ever imagine or make of ourselves. And because we know that he will never stop working with us until he has molded us to our perfect capacity, we can have the patience to love and accept ourselves as he continues to fashion us.

> Ye cannot behold with your natural eyes, for the present time, the designs of your God concerning those things which shall come hereafter, and the glory which shall follow after much tribulation (D&C 58:3).

3. *The relationship of a child to its parent*

The obedient and submissive relationship of a young child to its wiser, more responsible parent is obvious. This example has been used repeatedly to teach submission to God. In Mosiah 3:19, for example, we learn that part of losing our "natural man" and being born again as new creatures in Christ is to become "as a child." This counsel is one of the major themes in scripture.

> Except ye be converted, and become as little children, ye shall not enter into the kingdom of heaven (Matt. 18:3).

We should remember that of all the names he could have taught us to use, the Lord most preferred the name of "Father." This explains much about our intended relationship.

> Therefore, whoso repenteth and cometh unto me as a little child, him will I receive, for of such is the kingdom of God (3 Ne. 9:22).

4. *The relationship of a sheep to its shepherd*

No one but the proud and arrogant would dare to suggest that a sheep could ever care for itself as well as the loving shepherd.

> O ye workers of iniquity; ye that are puffed up in the vain things of the world, ye that have professed to have known the ways of righteousness nevertheless have gone astray, as sheep having no shepherd, notwithstanding a shepherd hath called after you and is still calling after you, but ye will not hearken unto his voice!
>
> Behold, I say unto you, that the good shepherd doth call you; yea, and in his own name he doth call you, which is the name of Christ; and if ye will not hearken unto the voice of the good shepherd, to the name by which ye are called, behold, ye are not the sheep of the good shepherd. (Alma 5:37-38.)

Life presents constant opposition to our righteous goals

and desires. On every hand we encounter enemies and evil forces which try to destroy us. The self-willed, independent sheep faces all this alone, with no resource but himself. But the submissive sheep, who yields and trusts his keeping to the Great and Wise Shepherd, is promised a table of plenty in the very presence of his enemies (See Ps. 23:5). His head is annointed, and the cup of his blessings "runneth over" because he has yielded himself to the Great "Shepherd and Bishop of our souls" (1 Pet. 2:25), who said that he came to bless the submissive with a more abundant and successful life than could ever be found in the conceit of their own self-will.

> And now I say unto you that the good shepherd doth call after you; and if you will hearken unto his voice he will bring you into his fold, and ye are his sheep. . . (Alma 5:60).
>
> Know ye that the Lord he is God: it is he that hath made us, and not we ourselves; we are his people, and the sheep of his pasture (Ps. 100:3).

5. *The relationship of a branch to its vine*

> I am the true vine, and my Father is the husbandman.
>
> I am the vine, ye are the branches: He that abideth in me, and I in him, the same bringeth forth much fruit: *for without me ye can do nothing.*
>
> Abide in me, and I in you. As the branch cannot bear fruit of itself, except it abide in the vine; no more can ye, except ye abide in me. (John 15:1, 5, 4.)

This is, perhaps, the most compelling of all the examples the Lord has given. To further emphasize the necessity of this submissive, yielding relationship, the Savior warned, "If a man abide not in me, he is cast forth as a branch, and is withered; and men gather them, and cast them into the fire, and they are burned" (John 15:6). Again in the latter days, he warned, "And if any man shall seek to build up himself, and seeketh not my counsel, he shall have no power, and his folly shall be made manifest" (D&C 136:19).

Each of these five examples was designed by God to assure us that submission to him is not a passive, apathetic dwindling into nothingness, but an exciting partnership in which we become more through him than we could ever become by ourselves.

6. *The Savior's life*

Abinadi prophesied of the example which Jesus would give, "the will of the Son being swallowed up in the will of the Father" (Mosiah 15:7). The Lord often drew our attention to his example of submission to the Father. "For I came down from heaven, not to do mine own will, but the will of him that sent me" (John 6:38). "I can of mine own self do nothing . . . because I seek not mine own will, but the will of the Father which hath sent me" (John 5:30).

But the Savior also wanted us to know that it is natural to waver as our resolves weaken in times of stress. The Lord never once faltered in submitting his will to the Father, until he reached the Garden of Gethsemane, and there, even he, the greatest of all, wavered under the crushing weight of our sins. So that we understand that no one is condemned for having such feelings, he caused this most astonishing part of his life to be recorded in detail.

As the Lord approached the final moments of his life, as he entered into the actual accomplishment of the atonement, offering himself as the sacrifice for our sins, the great Jehovah, the sinless Savior, actually stumbled and faltered. Our perfect, flawless Savior felt dread and weakness, and he wanted this most important fact recorded in the description of his life!

Until this moment, Jesus Christ had never experienced the effects of personal sin. What he knew about sin must have come second hand. Not once in his entire life had he ever felt a moment of guilt, shame, or unworthiness before the Father. Thus, as he began, for the first time to actually feel and experience the effects of sin, as he began to feel the guilt and shame and the pure horror of our sins, the same as if he had committed them, he began "to be sore amazed, and to be very heavy" (Mark 14:33), and he said to his apostles, "My soul is exceeding sorrowful, even unto death" (Matt. 26:38).

No mortal words can convey the agony which he suffered, but we do know that his experience was not a picturesque, idealistic, peaceful kneeling at the side of a rock as we so often see portrayed in art. The scriptures reveal that his agony was so great that "he went a little farther, and *fell on his face,* and prayed," saying these words:

> O my Father, if it be possible, let this cup pass from me: nevertheless not as I will, but as thou wilt (Matt. 26:39).

The incomprehensible weight and agony of bearing the punishment for our sins was so great that not even Jesus could accomplish it in one short session. Three times he rose from the terrible anguish and returned to the sleepy apostles. Three times he went, alone, to feel and to suffer and to atone for us. Three times he cried out to the Father for deliverance from the agony of that awful pain crushing down upon him. Three times he expressed his fear and dread and wavering, "saying the same words:"

> O my Father, if this cup may not pass away from me, except I drink it, thy will be done (Matt. 26:42).

Now we must ask why the Savior, who came to show us the perfect example of holiness and submission to the Father, would want us to know that there, in the garden, "even God, the greatest of all," trembled and wavered, "and would that I might not drink the bitter cup, and shrink" (D&C 19:18). There are at least three reasons that he wanted us to know of his desire for escape.

First, when our mortal weaknesses cause us to waver, to tremble and shrink from our responsibilities, we can remember that he also had those same feelings. Jesus wants us to understand that there is neither shame nor disgrace in having the desire to quit, or to escape the challenges we encounter. Not as long, that is, as we endure to the end and continue to pray, in spite of our feelings, "nevertheless not my will, but thine be done."

Secondly, Jesus was not denied the help for which he asked. An angel appeared, "strengthening him" (Luke 22:43). Therefore, we should realize that when our feelings are pulling us away from our duty, we too, will be given help to endure. Joseph Smith counselled us to abandon our pride, admit our need, and ask for his help.

> Help thy servants to say, *with thy grace assisting them:*
> Thy will be done, O Lord, and not ours (D&C 109:44).

If the Lord himself had to cry out for help, why should we be ashamed of our need?

The third message of this sacred account is that we should be totally honest with God about our feelings. The Savior did not fake the garden experience. He was in agony, and he found himself shrinking from his duty, but he was honest enough and humble enough to tell his Father how he felt. He certainly did not want to feel that way, so he asked for help. If we are hurting, if our commitment is weakening, we should say so. Jesus did. Why should we allow our foolish pride to try to hide our real feelings from God? He already knows them, and he understands. He did not condemn Jesus, nor count his wavering as sin. Rather, he sent help to strengthen his resolve and to keep him in the line of his duty, and that is exactly what he will do for us when our hearts are submissive before him.

XI
Trusting In God

A Basis For Trust

In the Bible we are told that our "faith should not stand in the wisdom of men, but in the power of God" (1 Cor. 2:5). If, at this moment, we are hurting and our life is not arranged as we would like, on what basis can we increase our trust in God? Let us consider five reasons why it is logical and rational to trust him.

1. ***God is always good.***

> The Lord is good, a stronghold in the day of trouble; and he knoweth them that trust in him (Nahum 1:7).

Armed with the confidence that God is *always* good and that he will *always* give good things to us when properly and worthily asked, we will not be able to doubt him or his love, regardless of the circumstances in which we find ourselves. To know God is to trust him, for "His goodness stands approved, unchanged from day to day . . ." (Hymns No. 67).

2. ***God will never allow anything ultimately "bad" to happen.***

> And we know that *all things* work together for good to them that love God . . . (Rom. 8:28).

> . . . all things shall work together for your good, if ye walk uprightly . . . (D&C 90:24).
>
> Therefore, let your hearts be comforted; for all things shall work together for good to them that walk uprightly . . . (D&C 100:15).

What wonderful promises these are! We should fervently cling to them. We, who see and evaluate circumstances with our short-sighted, mortal vision, have in these three verses the promise that if we truly love and obey God, he will somehow turn *everything* which happens in our lives to our good and our growth. Will we understand how it is to be so? Probably not. But will we believe and expect it and tell him so in our prayers? Yes! Because we know that we can trust him to bring good out of every circumstance, no matter how it may hurt at the moment.

> God moves in a mysterious way
> His wonders to perform;
> He plants his footsteps in the sea
> And rides upon the storm.
>
> Ye fearful Saints fresh courage take;
> The clouds ye so much dread
> Are big with mercy and shall break
> In blessings on your head.
>
> Judge not the Lord by feeble sense,
> But trust him for his grace;
> Behind a frowning providence
> He hides a smiling face.
>
> Blind belief is sure to err
> and scan his works in vain;
> God is his own interpreter,
> And he will make it plain.
>
> ("God Moves in a Mysterious Way," Hymns No. 48.)

3. *God constantly looks for opportunities to bless us.*

> For the eyes of the Lord run to and fro throughout the whole earth, to shew himself strong in the behalf of them whose heart is perfect toward him (2 Chr. 16:9).

> For thus saith the Lord—I, the Lord . . . delight to honor those who serve me in righteousness and in truth unto the end (D&C 76:5).

Having searched the world for those who are serving him in righteousness, the Lord then "delights" to bestow honor upon them through his attention, blessings, grace, and friendship. The blessings, he says, are not reserved for those who are already perfect, but for "those who love me and keep all my commandments, *and him that seeketh so to do . . ." (D&C 46:9).*

4. *God desires to bless us with good health and success.*

> Beloved, I wish above all things that thou mayest prosper and be in health, even as thy soul prospereth (3 John 1:2).

Not only does God delight to honor and bless us, but he wants us to enjoy good health and prosperity "above all things."

> And behold, all that he requires of you is to keep his commandments; and he has promised you that if ye would keep his commandments ye should prosper . . . (Mosiah 2:22).

It is proper to ask God for success, prosperity, and health, and to trust God for their fulfillment (in his own time and in his own way) as we continue to work toward those goals, because he has already promised that this is his desire for us.

5. *God has proven himself in the past.*

Because God never changes, perhaps no other exercise can be so instrumental in diminishing our doubts and fears as reviewing God's goodness in the past. How can we possibly doubt him when we pause to remember the many things he has already done in our own lives and in the lives of others?

> We doubt not the Lord nor his goodness
> We've proved him in days that are past . . .
> ("We Thank Thee Oh God For A Prophet," Hymns No. 196.)

Trusting In Spite Of Outward Circumstances

When we are deciding whether or not we will trust God, we are often influenced by what we think we know about our circumstances. We usually call this "being realistic." The problem with limiting our faith and trust in God to what *we* think our circumstances would allow him to do for us, is that we do not see into the future as he does. Consequently, by failing to trust in his superior knowledge and power to influence our circumstances, we cheat ourselves.

Of course, it is easy to trust him when our "seen realities"[9] have everything going our way. For instance, once the Red Sea had opened and half the camp of Israel had passed through safely, it would have been rather easy to trust God to allow us through also. But the real trust comes *before* God has revealed his means of deliverance to us. What he wants to know, and what we must decide, is will we trust him in the dark as well as in the light? Will we trust him even when he steps aside temporarily and it seems as though he

---

[9]This wonderful phrase is borrowed from Stephen R. Covey's book, *Spiritual Roots of Human Relations.*

doesn't care? "Trust in him at all times; ye people . . ." (Ps. 62:8). One of the important principles of receiving grace is in learning to trust God "at all times," especially when we haven't the slightest idea how he might accomplish the object of our need.

I have learned that God is delighted with the opportunity to manifest his power in our behalf when our trust is complete and unwavering. But, to enjoy the miracles of his great power, we must first manifest to him our conviction that his best judgment will always be done, and that we trust his good will toward us—no matter how detrimental our circumstances may seem.

> To my understanding, the Lord is telling us that our attitude or frame of mind, heart, and spirit is of crucial importance in releasing the true power of prayer. While this seems obvious, I believe it not to be very common. *Too often we place our faith in the seen realities rather than in the unseen God and his promises to us.* We then call ourselves realistic, but with the Lord nothing is impossible: if the thing we request is right—that is, if it is wise from the Lord's point of view, even though all the seen realities might shout at us that it cannot be done—and if we pray in faith, believing that it can be done and that it is right, and then put ourself in alliance with God in doing our part, the Lord will work his miracles. *I have come to believe from my own experiences that many times faith in the Lord Jesus Christ just begins when 'it cannot be done,' when all of the seen realities combine together to hedge up the way, and people mock, and ridicule.* (Stephen R. Covey, *Spiritual Roots of Human Relations,* S.L.C., Utah: Deseret Book Co., 1970 pp.173-174; emphasis added.)

When we fully trust the Lord, we do not worry about all the possible consequences of our choices. Rather, we simply go the way we know is right, trusting in him, knowing that he is a God of power, and that his divine purposes will be fulfilled. When we trust the Lord and draw near to him in our tribulations, he responds by drawing near to us. And, by so doing, we will come to treasure adversity as one of our most valued experiences.

> Draw near unto me and I will draw near unto you; seek me diligently and ye shall find me . . . (D&C 88:63).

The Example Of Abraham's Trust

Abraham is a great example of the kind of faith and trust we have been considering. We remember that he was about one hundred years old when he was promised a son through whose lineage an innumerable posterity would come. While it is true that people lived longer in those days, the fact does not diminish the magnitude of Abraham's trust in God because it is also true that Abraham considered his body and Sarah's womb as good as dead. His "seen realities" were years and years of barrenness, now seemingly sealed in permanence by wrinkled old bodies. Yet we know that, ignoring these "seen realities," he did not even question the unlikelihood of God's promise.

> [Abraham] Who against hope believed in hope . . .
>
> And being not weak in faith, *he considered not* his own body now dead, when he was about an hundred years old, neither yet the deadness of Sarah's womb:
>
> *He staggered not* at the promise of God through unbelief; but was strong in faith, giving glory to God;
>
> And *being fully persuaded* that, what he had promised, he was able also to perform. (Rom. 4:18-21.)

The scriptures record the marvelous bestowal of grace and power and honor that came to Abraham because of his faith and trust. Abraham's example of trust is recorded in scripture for our benefit, not as a history lesson, but to teach us to strive for similar confidence. Can we develop enough trust in God to prevent us from worrying over the "seen realities" which, from our limited perspective, seem to be in the way of God's miracles?

The Example Of Peter's Trust

We often think of Peter as untrustworthy because he denied the Savior three times, but we do Peter an injustice for so thinking. Perhaps we should try walking on water before we are so eager to judge him.

There was another experience in Peter's life which teaches a great lesson about trusting God. Jesus was speaking to the crowds near the seashore. Anxious to hear him, the multitude kept pushing forward until Jesus was nearly forced into the water. The Lord turned, and seeing Peter and his boat close by, he asked permission to enter the boat to complete his sermon.

At the conclusion of the sermon, Jesus turned again to Peter and suggested that they push out to sea and go fishing. This suggestion frustrated Peter. He had spent his whole life fishing there in the Sea of Galilee. He was a skilled and successful fisherman, and he knew that one had to let down the nets in the darkness of night, when the fish felt safe to come to the surface. Peter had been fishing all night, and had not caught a single fish. He was not anxious to repeat the failure.

Such were Peter's "seen realities." Everything in his experience told him that to let down the nets in broad daylight would be a complete waste of time. So how did he respond? Did he trust the Lord or did he doubt? Both. Peter was honest with the Lord. He protested and admitted his doubt, but he also expressed trust and willingness to obey the Master in spite of his doubt.

> Now when he had left speaking, he said unto Simon, Launch out into the deep, and let down your nets for a draught.
>
> And Simon answering said unto him, Master, we have toiled all the night, and have taken nothing: *nevertheless at thy word I will let down the net.* (Luke 5:4-5.)

In other words, Peter was learning that when God tells us to do something which seems contrary to our own perception of reality, his word alone should be reason enough to obey. And what was the result of his trust? A truly great lesson, for "when they had this done, they enclosed a great multitude of fishes" (Luke 5:6).

This was a rich reward indeed, and a fitting symbol of the rewards we, too, will reap by placing our trust in the Lord. So great was their catch that Peter had to call for help from his partner's ship. When they had finally loaded all the fish, both boats were so full that they almost sank!

It would seem that Luke included this interesting "fish story" in his account of the Savior's mortal life because the story is not really about fish, but about the kinds of rewards we reap when we trust God in spite of our "seen realities."

The Arm Of Flesh

We all encounter times when we desperately need added strength or knowledge, understanding, wisdom, insight, or other kinds of help. These are times when we know we simply cannot handle the situation facing us on our own. The choice which faces us at these times is simple; it is a black and white choice. Either we choose to trust in God and rely on his grace—which we cannot control—or we choose to rely on the resources of men—which we can control. Choosing the strength and resources of men in preference to God's help is known in the scriptures as "relying on the arm of flesh." The Lord has made it plain that those who so choose will be cursed by their choice.

> O Lord, I have trusted in thee, and I will trust in thee forever. I will not put my trust in the arm of flesh; for I know that cursed is he that putteth his trust in the arm of flesh. Yea, cursed is he that putteth his trust in man or maketh flesh his arm. (2 Ne. 4:34; see also 2 Ne. 28:31.)

> Wo to them that go down to Egypt for help; and stay on horses, and trust in chariots, because they are many; and in horsemen, because they are very strong; but *they look not unto the Holy One of Israel,* neither seek the Lord (Isa. 31:1)!

The "Holy One of Israel" is the Lord Jesus Christ, who has invited us to come unto him for peace, for help, and for everything we need. When we have our back against the wall, and we just can't make it on our own, let us not "go down to Egypt." Let us go to the Lord, "for behold he is mightier than all the earth, then why not mightier than Laban and his fifty, yea, or even than his tens of thousands?" (1 Ne. 4:1). When we trust in "the arm of flesh" instead of the Lord, our relationship with him is weakened. Where will we go the next time we need help?

"It is better to trust in the Lord than to put confidence in man" (Ps. 118:8). Why is it better? Because it does not matter to him what our problems are; it doesn't matter to him how deeply entrenched we are in our problems, or how limited our resources are, because his power is infinite, and "there is no restraint to the Lord to save by many or by few" (1 Sam. 14:6).

The Lord already has a "way out" prepared for us if we will only give him the chance to demonstrate his stubborn love. He is so anxious to bless us, but he will never impose himself on us against our will. Let us avoid offending him through the substitution of the "arm of flesh."

"Yet Will I Trust In Him"

> Trust in the Lord with all thine heart; and lean not unto thine own understanding.
>
> In all thy ways acknowledge him, and he shall direct thy paths. (Prov. 3:5-6).

What better reason could we have for trusting God than the promise of his personal guidance? We have shared the words of the Lord concerning our trust in him versus trusting in ourselves and in the resources of the world. We have emphasized that our choice is simple; we choose either A or B, black or white. There is no room in between. Either we trust him or we don't. If we are not willing to trust him for everything, then we really don't trust him at all. I repeat, if we are not willing to trust him at all times and in all circumstances, how can we claim to trust him in anything?

> . . . he that believeth not God hath made him a liar; because he believeth not the record that God gave of his Son (1 Jn. 5:10).

> Throughout the Church hundreds of thousands of faithful Saints have truly consecrated their lives and their energies to the work of the Lord, secure in the assurance that thereby they please him.
>
> It is a disappointment, however, to find many others who are not willing to trust the Lord—or to trust in his promise when he says, "Prove me and see." I often wonder why men cannot trust their Lord . . . He has promised his children every blessing contingent upon their faithfulness, *but fickle man places his trust in "the arm of flesh" and sets about to make his own way unaided by him who could do so much.* (Spencer W. Kimball, as quoted in the 1974-75 Melchizedek Priesthood Manual, *When Thou Art Converted, Strengthen Thy Brethren,* p. 86; emphasis added.)

Learning to trust God is a wonderful and rewarding adventure, but it often involves some real growing pains. The Lord understands why it is hard for us to let go of the things we can see and control, so that we may place our trust in him. When we have such doubts, he wants us to discuss them with him.

As I worked my way back from excommunication I was full of doubt, and I went to him repeatedly to find the faith and reassurance that would sustain me through my problems. Through the process of my conversion, however, I learned for myself that he responds kindly to an honest prayer such as, "Heavenly Father, I know that I am weak. I have so many doubts, but I really do want to believe. I want to trust. I am willing to learn. I am willing to wait. Please help me to overcome my doubts."

> The Lord is my light and my salvation; whom shall I fear? the Lord is the strength of my life; of whom shall I be afraid?
>
> Though an host should encamp against me, my heart shall not fear . . . (Ps. 27:1, 3.)
>
> Though he slay me, yet will I trust in him (Job 13:15).

XII

A Sure Foundation

Christ-Centered Or Self-Centered?

Where do we look for help when troubles afflict us? Where do we look when we desire spiritual improvement? The counsel we have been given is to "look" unto Christ as the center and foundation of our lives.

> Behold, I am the law, and the light. *Look unto me,* and endure to the end, and ye shall live . . . (3 Ne. 15:9).
>
> Hearken to me, ye that follow after righteousness, ye that seek the Lord: *look unto the rock* from whence ye are hewn . . . (Isa. 51:1; see also 2 Ne. 8:1).

Unless we live close to the Savior, looking toward him can be difficult because there are so many other sources to which we can look for guidance, strength, and help in our problems. The world is filled with books, self-improvement and behavioral modification programs, and counselors to which we may look for our needs. Nevertheless, it is only when we learn to look to Jesus Christ for the true light and resources we need that we will achieve the peace, success, and abundance in life that he meant us to have. Isaiah warned that "wo" would befall those who look elsewhere, trusting in the more obvious arm of flesh, instead of relying upon Jesus Christ.

> Wo to them that go down to Egypt for help; and stay on horses, and trust in chariots, because they are many; and in horsemen, because they are very strong; *but they look not unto the Holy One of Israel,* neither seek the Lord! (Isa. 31:1; see also Isa. 45:21-22).

> And we talk of Christ, we rejoice in Christ, we preach of Christ, we prophesy of Christ, and we write according to our prophecies, *that our children may know to what source they may look* for a remission of their sins (2 Ne. 25:26).

As the "natural man" strives for survival and success, it is normal for him to center his thoughts and emotions, his confidence and his reliance upon himself. We should realize, however, that this self-centered philosophy was one of the main points of the anti-Christ doctrine preached by Korihor and others like him. Korihor taught that reliance upon Jesus Christ "is the effect of a frenzied mind; and this derangement of your minds," he said, "comes because of the traditions of your fathers, which lead you away into a belief of things which are not so" (Alma 30:16). As he went about teaching people to rely solely upon themselves rather than upon Christ, he taught the popular and appealing humanistic doctrine that "every man fared in this life according to the management of the creature; therefore every man prospered according to his genius, and that every man conquered according to his [own] strength" (Alma 30:17).

Do not misunderstand. It is necessary that we use our own strengths and abilities to do as much for ourselves as we can. But it is also imperative that we recognize that no one can ever do enough, by his efforts alone, to live the obedient life that will result in exaltation. If we could, why would we need the Savior? Consider the following words from the 1969-70 Gospel Doctrine Manual.

> "I am the Way," the Savior tells those who hope to find the means, the way to create heaven. *Only in him can any man find the strength, the power and ability to live a godly*

> *life. Only in Christ is there power to transform the human mind and the human heart . . . Only in Jesus Christ can any man learn the truth of what he is and how he can be changed from what he is to do the good for which he hopes.* (In His Footsteps Today, S.L.C., Utah: Deseret Sunday School Union, 1969, p. 4; emphasis added.)
>
> Only Jesus Christ is uniquely qualified to provide that hope, that confidence, and that strength to overcome the world and rise above our human failings ("Jesus Christ: Our Savior and Redeemer," Ezra Taft Benson, *Ensign*, November 1983, p. 6.)

As we mature spiritually, we learn that to achieve true success, our self-centeredness must be surrendered to a Christ-centeredness. He has told us that he is our only path to the Father (John 14:6). While we continue to use all the wisdom, strengths, and abilities with which we have been blessed, we still must learn to rely upon Christ for the resources which will lead us back to the Father. We must learn to build our entire life upon the foundation of Jesus Christ. Brigham Young referred to this process of surrender and change of foundations as "the greatest and most important of all requirements!"

> The greatest and most important of all requirements of our Father in Heaven and of his Son Jesus Christ . . . is to believe in Jesus Christ, confess him, seek to know him, cling to him, make friends with him. Take a course to open and keep open a communication with your elder brother or file leader—our Savior. (*Journal of Discourses,* Vol. 8, p. 339, as quoted in the Relief Society Manual, 1982, p. 24.)

The Apostle John also emphasized the paramount importance of making the Savior the foundation of our life. He focused this doctrine more clearly for us when he said, "He that hath the Son hath life; and he that hath not the Son of God hath not life" (1 Jn. 5:12). This short and concise statement is of utmost importance. It clarifies the seeming complexities we find in the circumstances of life. John is telling us that all success and failure, all problems and situations which lift us or which pull us down are rooted in the simple truth that everything we attempt to do in life is inseparably connected to our relationship with Jesus Christ. If the Savior is our example and the center of our attention and foundation of our values and actions, all things are going to work together for our good (see Rom. 8:28). But if we place other things ahead of his importance in our lives, we are going to have continual problems and frustrations. How often we cheat ourselves by trying to choose something in between. I know of no other example which so vividly illustrates the unfortunate tragedy and wasteful loss that is ours when we fail to center our lives on the Savior than the following vision:

> You remember that the Prophet [Joseph Smith] saw in panoramic vision at least nine of the Twelve in a foreign land. He saw them gathered in a circle, without shoes, beaten, tattered, discouraged. Standing above them in the air was the Lord Jesus Christ. And it was made known to the Prophet that Christ yearned to show himself to them, to reach down and lift them. But they did not see him. The Savior looked upon them and wept. We are told by two of the brethren who heard Joseph rehearse that vision that he could never speak of it without weeping himself. Why? Why should he be so touched? Because Christ willingly came to the earth so that all the Father's family could come to him boldly, knowing that he knows what is taking place in us when we sin, that he knows all our feelings and cares. *The greatest tragedy of life is that, having paid that awful price of suffering "according to the flesh that his bowels might be filled with compassion,"* (see Alma 7:11-13) *and being now prepared to reach down and help us, he is forbidden because we won't let him. We look down instead of up.* (Truman G. Madsen, *The Highest In Us,* 1st Ed., S.L.C., Utah: Bookcraft, Inc., 1978, p. 85; emphasis added.)

By "His Merits" Or Ours?

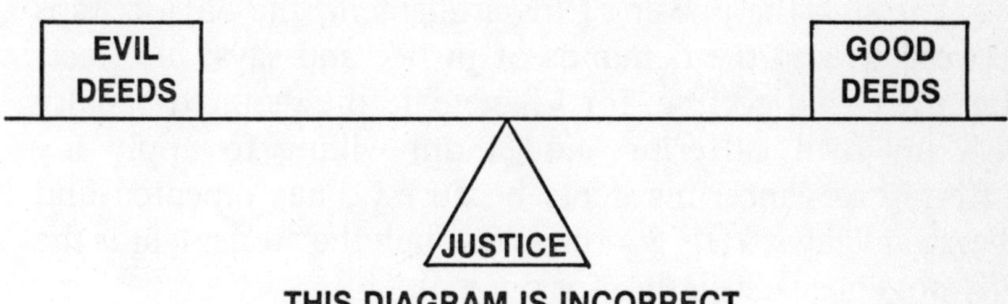

THIS DIAGRAM IS INCORRECT

Many people are deceived by the belief that their own good works can balance the scales of justice, or even tip it in their favor. They feel that somehow, as long as the good deeds in their lives outweigh the evil, they will prosper in the day of judgment. While it is appealing, this concept is false and very deceiving.

The truth is that justice does not allow our good deeds to cancel our evil deeds. Justice demands that every good deed be rewarded, and that every evil deed be punished. Every act stands alone, in harmony with the law, or out of harmony, but alone it stands, independent of all other deeds. Beyond the atonement, there is no debit/credit system in God's plan of justice. Since justice demands a full payment (punishment) for every violation of God's laws, God, in his perfection, can never override justice with mercy. To remain a perfect God, he must always honor and execute perfect justice—with no exceptions. That is why we would all be condemned to a state of hell and to an eternity of punishment were it not for the grace and atonement of Jesus Christ which rescues us from that damnation.

While justice does demand that the penalty be paid for every sin, the law of mercy will permit Jesus to pay that penalty in our stead. He alone has the right to stand before justice as our substitute. Thus, through his grace, we may become justified, while no amount of good works that we perform could ever pay or compensate for our sins.

Through the power of his atonement, the Savior steps between us and the demands of justice and says, in effect, "Let my friend go free, for I have paid the required penalty with my own suffering, and I am willing to apply my suffering to cancel his debts because he has repented and obeyed my laws." His goodness through the atonement is the only possible cancellation for our evil.

> Behold, he offereth himself a sacrifice for sin, to answer the ends of the law, unto all those who have a broken heart and a contrite spirit; and unto none else [not even the doers of good works] can the ends of the law be answered (2 Ne. 2:7).

Lehi stressed this message of dependence upon the merits of Christ as our only way back to the Father when he said, "Wherefore, how great [is] the importance to make these things known unto the inhabitants of the earth, that they may know that *there is no flesh that can dwell in the presence of God, save it be through the merits, and mercy, and grace of the Holy Messiah* . . . (2 Ne. 2:8). When Enoch understood this principle, he said to the Lord, ". . . thou hast made me, and given unto me a right to thy throne, *and not of myself, but through thine own grace* . . ." (Moses 7:59). The great Nephite missionary, Aaron, bore a similar testimony: "And since man had fallen he could not merit anything of himself . . ." (Alma 22:14).

> But after that the kindness and love of God our Savior toward man appeared.
>
> *Not by works of righteousness which we have done,* but according to his mercy he saved us, by the washing of regeneration, and renewing of the Holy Ghost;
>
> Which he shed on us abundantly through Jesus Christ our Savior;
>
> *That being justified by his grace,* we should be made

heirs according to the hope of eternal life. (Titus 3:4-7; see also Rom. 11:5-6.)

In the foregoing scripture the Apostle Paul teaches that it is impossible for us to become justified before God by our own "works of righteousness." That his doctrine is true was testified by Lehi, when he said, "And men are instructed sufficiently that they know good from evil. And the law is given unto men. *And by the law no flesh is justified* . . ." (2 Ne. 2:5.)

How often we deceive ourselves by trying to substitute our own works for the merits of his grace. It is impossible through good works alone to accumulate enough merit to obligate our exaltation. The celestial kingdom is not obtained through the acummulation of "merit badges" as is done to become an Eagle Scout. There is no parallel between the two objectives.

> For by grace are ye saved through faith; and that not of yourselves: it is the gift of God:
>
> Not of works, lest any man should boast. (Eph. 2:8-9.)

It is at this point that many good people stumble over Christ. "What about our good works?" they protest. "Don't they count for anything? What about our blessings being predicated upon obedience to the irrevocably decreed laws, etc.?" (See D&C 130:20; 82:10; 132:5 for example.) Does the importance of grace mean that our works do not count? Of course not. It is preposterous to suppose that the God who said we will be judged and rewarded according to our works cares only for our belief and not our deeds.

> For God is not unrighteous to forget your work and labour of love, which ye have shewed toward his name . . . (Heb. 6:10).

The value of our works is not invalidated by our need to rely upon the merits of Christ. There is no competition between grace and works. Study, obedience, and service are as essential to progress and exaltation as is Christ's grace. They are intended to work together. The Savior's grace will do far more for the person who is engaged in building the kingdom than it can for the one who is trying to merely believe himself into heaven.

To those who insist on trying to reach heaven on the ladder of their good works alone, Paul said, "Christ is become of no effect unto you, whosoever of you are [trying to be] justified by the law; ye are fallen from grace" (Gal. 5:4). Paul and the other prophets we have quoted were not teaching that good works are improper, nor were they saying that they are not important or necessary. What they were trying to emphasize is that notwithstanding the value of our good deeds, we are still entirely dependent upon the merits of the atonement of Jesus Christ if we are to be redeemed. They want us to realize that if we ignore the role of Christ's grace and cling to our good works instead, we are choosing to rely upon our own merits instead of relying upon the merits of Jesus Christ and his grace. Hence, we are fallen far below the righteousness and holiness that we could have attained through the proper relationship with the Savior.

We are told in modern revelation that one of the principle reasons for the bringing forth of the Book of Mormon was to teach man to let go of his self-reliance and to learn to "rely upon the merits of Jesus Christ."

> . . . and that they might know the promises of the Lord, *and that they may believe the gospel and rely upon the merits of Jesus Christ,* and be glorified through faith in his name, and that through their repentance they might be saved. Amen. (D&C 3:20.)

In the 1969-70 Gospel Doctrine manual we read:

> Those founded on the rock are the only ones who will successfully meet the tests ahead. By building faith through their trials *they will reach a point in life where they rely completely upon God.* (*In His Footsteps Today,* S.L.C., Utah: Deseret Sunday School Union, 1969, p. 37; emphasis added.)

Nephi taught us to "feast upon the words of Christ;" giving as the reason that "the words of Christ will tell you all things what ye should do" (2 Ne. 32:3). Hugh W. Pinnock of the First Council of Seventy has said:

> . . . we function best in an environment of freedom. We are free when we are independent, and *we are totally independent only when we are completely dependent upon the Savior (Devotional Speeches of the Year,* Provo, Utah: Brigham Young University Press, 1979, p. 116; emphasis added).
>
> Faith in him is more than mere acknowledgment that he lives. It is more than professing belief. *Faith in Jesus Christ consists of complete reliance on Him.* ("Jesus Christ: Our Savior and Redeemer," Ezra Taft Benson, *Ensign,* November 1983, p. 8; emphasis added.)

"A Sure Foundation"

The Savior introduced the concept of making him the foundation of our lives by drawing a comparison between the wise man who "built his house upon a rock" by obedience to his words, and the foolish man who ignored the Savior's commandments (or only gave lip service to them) and thereby "built his house upon the sand."

> Therefore, whoso heareth these sayings of mine and doeth them, I will liken him unto a wise man, who built his house upon a rock—
>
> And the rain descended, and the floods came, and the winds blew, and beat upon that house; and it fell not, for it was founded upon a rock.

> And everyone that heareth these sayings of mine and doeth them not shall be likened unto a foolish man, who built his house upon the sand—
>
> And the rain descended, and the floods came, and the winds blew, and beat upon that house; and it fell, and great was the fall of it. (3 Ne. 14:24-27.)

The comparison between the safety and strength of building upon rock instead of sand is obvious. What we do not always realize, however, is that this analogy illustrates the contrast between the Christ-centered life and trying to make our own way. The rock that Jesus referred to was not a physical rock, but the Savior himself.

> And now, my sons, remember, remember that it is upon the rock of our Redeemer, who is Christ, the Son of God, that ye must build your foundation . . . (Hel. 5:12).

> For other foundation can no man lay than that [which] is laid, which is Jesus Christ (1 Cor. 3:11).

> By acquiring faith in the Lord Jesus Christ a person has assured for his life the rocklike base that will support the structure against storms.
>
> It is possible to obtain some blessings from heaven, by faith, without accepting the true message of salvation. [but] *To be founded on the rock means a complete acceptance of Christ, with resulting obedience to the principles and ordinances of the gospel.* (1969-70 Gospel Doctrine Manual, *In His Footsteps Today,* S.L.C., Utah: Deseret Sunday School Union, 1969, p. 34-35; emphasis added.)

Those who make Christ their life-center and foundation and then live in obedience to his gospel, are guaranteed exaltation. Guaranteed! As "the Rock of Heaven," Christ's power is as "broad as eternity." This is to say that no event, no sin, no weakness, nothing shall be strong enough to overcome those who truly make Jesus "the way" that they follow.

> . . . I am Messiah, the King of Zion, the Rock of Heaven, which is broad as eternity; *whoso cometh in at the gate and climbeth up by me shall never fall* . . . (Moses 7:53).

> And now, my sons, remember, remember that it is upon the rock of our Redeemer, who is Christ, the Son of God, that ye must build your foundation; that when the devil shall send forth his mighty winds, yea, his shafts in the whirlwind, yea, when all his hail and his mighty storm shall beat upon you, *it shall have no power over you* to drag you down to the gulf of misery and endless wo, *because of the rock upon which ye are built, which is a sure foundation, a foundation whereon if men build they cannot fall* (Hel. 5:12).

Paul said, "the foundation of God standeth sure, having this seal, The Lord knoweth them that are his" (2 Tim. 2:19). He also taught that Jesus Christ "is able to keep you from falling, and to present you faultless before the presence of his glory with exceeding joy" (Jude 24). We cannot help but ask how this is possible. How can the foundation of Jesus Christ be so sure and tried that it can actually guarantee that we "shall not" and "cannot fall"? The Lord has not explained in any detail how he works this miracle, but he has answered our question with the assurance that all victory is made possible through his grace.

> And if you do these last commandments of mine, which I have given you, the gates of hell shall not prevail against you; *for my grace is sufficient for you,* and you shall be lifted up at the last day (D&C 17:8; see also D&C 18:31).

> . . . if ye shall deny yourselves of all ungodliness and love God with all your might, mind and strength, *then is his grace sufficient for you,* that by his grace ye may be perfect in Christ . . . (Moro. 10:32; see also Ether 12:26-27; 2 Cor. 12:7-10).

Could there be any greater reason to accept him as the center and foundation of our life? "But how does he make it happen?" we ask, as if we will refuse the gift until we can understand it. Must we allow our curiosity to interfere with our faith? We enjoy thousands of the benefits of science and medicine without understanding how their miracles occur. If we only apply the proper procedure, we can benefit from them as much as the doctor or scientist who understands the entire process. The same is true of the Savior's grace. Putting Christ at the center of our life is the required procedure. Victory, joy, fellowship with the Father and exaltation are the promised rewards. Since the Lord has not revealed the details of his marvelous workings, let us just accept them, trust in him and be grateful for the grace he offers us.

Will We Stumble Also?

Surrendering control of our life for a life that is lived in submission to the Will of God is often difficult for mortal man. We are taught by the world to be independent and self-sufficient. We are taught to make our own plans and to pursue our own goals. Such teachings are good, but when they are overemphasized, they can become the very obstacles that cause us to stumble over Christ and prevent him from becoming the foundation of our lives.

Paul said, "we preach Christ crucified, unto the Jews a stumbling block, and unto the Greeks foolishness" (1 Cor. 1:23). How careful we must be not to allow ourselves to stumble over the importance which Christ is meant to have in our lives.

> But Israel, which followed after the law of righteousness, hath not attained to the law of righteousness.
>
> Wherefore? Because they sought it not by faith, but as it were by the works of the law. For they stumbled at that stumblingstone;
>
> As it is written, *Behold, I lay in Sion a stumblingstone and rock of offence:* and whosoever believeth on him shall not be ashamed. (Rom. 9:31-33.)

> And now I, Jacob, am led on by the Spirit unto prophesying; for I perceive by the workings of the Spirit which is in me, that *by the stumbling of the Jews they will reject the stone upon which they might build and have safe foundation.*
>
> But behold, according to the scriptures, this stone shall become the great, and the last, and the only sure foundation, upon which the Jews can build. (Jacob 4:15-16.)

We have considered the need to place Jesus at the center of our lives. We have learned that Heavenly Father intended for everything in our life to revolve around the goal of becoming Christlike, for it was his mission to reveal the Father's nature to us. We have learned of the promises of success that are given for building our works upon the foundation of Christ, and that by so doing we can gain all the strength and grace required to fulfill every stewardship assigned to us.

At the beginning of this chapter we referred to Korihor's humanistic philosophy that mankind progresses and achieves solely upon the merits of each person's "genius" and "management." He referred to submissive reliance upon Jesus as "the effect of a frenzied mind" (Alma 30:16-17). Let us now compare his ideas to the inspired words of Elder Ezra Taft Benson, president of the Quorum of the Twelve Apostles.

> It was in Gethsemane where Jesus took on Himself the sins of the world, in Gethsemane where His pain was equivalent to the cumulative burden of all men, in Gethsemane where He descended below all things so that all could repent and come to Him.
>
> The mortal mind fails to fathom, the tongue cannot express, the pen of man cannot describe the breadth, depth, or height of the suffering of our Lord—or His infinite love for us.
>
> Yet there are those who arrogantly declare the most pernicious heresy, that the blood which extruded from the

physical body of our Lord on that night had no efficacy for the redemption of man. They would have you believe the only significance to Gethsemane was that Jesus made His decision there to go to the cross. They say that any suffering Jesus endured was only personal, not redemptive for the whole human race. *I know of no heresy more destructive to faith than this, for the individual who so accepts this delusion is beguiled to believe that he can achieve exaltation on the basis of his own merit, intelligence, and personal effort.*

Never forget, my young friends, that "it is by grace that we are saved, after all we can do." 2 Ne. 25:23 (Five Marks of the Divinity of Jesus Christ, *The New Era,* December 1980, pp. 47-48; emphasis added.)

Scripture – The Building Material For Our Foundation

How can we make Christ the foundation and center of our lives if we do not know who he is, what he is, how he feels about our situations and challenges, and how he would want us to respond to them? The Will of the Lord and the Word of the Lord are one and the same. We cannot know the Will of God for us unless we know the Word of God. How can we claim to have placed Christ at the center of our lives if we are ignorant of his word? How can we rely upon the Lord for strength and guidance in time of need if we do not know what he has promised in his scriptures to do for us? Neither the Father nor the Son will ever become familiar to us until we are familiar with their recorded words.

And whoso receiveth not my voice is not acquainted with my voice, and is not of me.

And by this you may know the righteous from the wicked . . . (D&C 84:52-53.)

I say unto you, I would that ye should remember to retain the name written always in your hearts, that ye are not found on the left hand of God, but that ye hear and know the voice by which ye shall be called, and also the name by which he shall call you.

For how knoweth a man the master whom he has not served, and who is a stranger unto him, and who is far from

> *the thoughts and intents of his heart?* (Mosiah 5:12-13.)

One of the most direct paths to improving our relationship with God lies in the prayerful study of his revealed word. Jesus indicated that he actually equates our feelings towards his scriptures to our feelings toward him when he said, "If a man love me, he will keep my words. . ." (John 14:23; see also 2 Ne. 28:29-30). Consider the words of Job, who said, "I have esteemed the words of his mouth more than my necessary food" (Job 23:12; see also 1 Pet. 2:2). Notice the emphasis that the Savior has placed upon making his word paramount in our daily life.

> Behold, I say unto you, that you must rely upon my word. . . (D&C 17:1; see also D&C 18:3).
>
> . . . he that hath the scriptures, let him search them. . . (3 Ne. 10:14; see also Mosiah 1:7).
>
> And I now give unto you a commandment to beware concerning yourselves, to *give diligent heed to the words of eternal life.* For you shall live by every word that proceedeth forth from the mouth of God. (D&C 84:43-44; see also Isa. 34:16; John 5:39.)

God's promises never fail. Everytime we obey his law, every time we make claim upon a promise we find in his word, every time we allow his word to be fulfilled in our life, we add another defeat to Satan and his hosts who chose to believe that God's word and plan would not work, and we bring glory to the God who spoke it.

> So shall my word be that goeth forth out of my mouth: *it shall not return unto me void, but it shall accomplish that which I please,* and it shall prosper in the thing whereto I sent it (Isa. 55:11).
>
> . . . and inasmuch as you keep my sayings *you shall not be confounded* in this world, nor in the world to come (D&C 93:52; see also 2 Tim. 3:16-17).

XIII

True Righteousness

There Is A Difference

All who truly seek after godliness would say that they are trying to be righteous, but how many of us can actually define what is meant by righteousness? The scriptures plainly differentiate between that true righteousness which is acceptable before God and the substitute, shortcut righteousness of man, which is not only insufficient to perfect us, but is, in many cases, detrimental to our progress.

In his preface to the Doctrine and Covanants, for example, the Lord referred to mankind's preference for their own ways instead of the Lord's righteousness as one of the reasons for the judgments and calamities which were about to fall upon the world.

> They seek not the Lord to establish *his righteousness, but every man walketh in his own way,* and after the image of his own God, whose image is in the likeness of the world. . . (D&C 1:16).

Joseph Smith taught that Satan uses man's false concepts of righteousness to confuse and restrain our progress. "All the religious world is boasting of righteousness: it is the doctrine of the devil to retard the human mind, and hinder our progress, by filling us with self-righteousness" (*Teachings of the Prophet Joseph Smith*, comp. Joseph Fielding Smith, 7th Ed., S.L.C., Utah: Deseret Book Co., 1951, p. 241). Paul also warned of the danger of substituting man's righteousness for the true righteousness of God:

> Brethren, my heart's desire and prayer to God for Israel is, that they might be saved.
>
> For I bear them record that they have a zeal of God, but not according to knowledge.
>
> For they *being ignorant of God's righteousness, and going about to establish their own righteousness,* have not submitted themselves unto the righteousness of God.
>
> For Christ is the end of the law for righteousness to every one that believeth. (Rom. 10:1-4.)

Wouldn't it be awful to discover that our zeal toward God had been without knowledge, and that all our "good works" and "church activity" had been with a zeal that was "ignorant of God's righteousness?"

Substituting Doing For Being

In the time of Christ, the Scribes and Pharisees were regarded by Israel as the very epitome of righteousness. Few have been as strict in their scrupulous obedience to every detail of the law. But Jesus emphatically declared that their imitation righteousness, their emphasis on outward deeds, was insufficient to gain entrance into heaven.

> For I say unto you, That except your righteousness shall exceed the righteousness of the scribes and Pharisees, ye shall in no case enter into the kingdom of heaven (Matt. 5:20).

God's true righteousness is Christ-centered, and places its emphasis on the things we are meant to become. It is rooted in the holiness which comes from faith in Jesus Christ and from following his example. Man's righteousness is self-centered and places its emphasis on self-sufficiency and the feelings we receive from the good works we do instead of the inward person we are meant to be. Man's righteousness is like having a check list of things to be done. And then, by definition, when we have complied with everything on the list, presto!—we are righteous. Paul often spoke of the difference between the righteousness of man, "which is of the law" and emphasizes things to do, and "the righteousness which is of God," emphasizing things to be.

> Yea doubtless, and I count all things but loss for the excellency of the knowledge of Christ Jesus my Lord: for whom I have suffered the loss of all things, and do count them but dung, that I may win Christ,
>
> And be found in him, *not having mine own righteousness,* which is of the law, but that [righteousness] which is through the faith of Christ, *the righteousness which is of God by faith:* (Philip. 3:8-9.)

The problem with man's outward, "check list" righteousness is that we tend to substitute doing for being. For example, it is completely possible to be in attendance at all church meetings without ever being inspired or changed. It is completely possible to pay an honest tithe and to give generously to the ward budget and fast offering funds from a sense of duty, without ever feeling a part in the growth and maintenance of God's kingdom. And it is quite possible to read hundreds of pages of scriptures and yet come away unaltered, no closer to the Lord than before the words were read. Each outward "good work" provides another item to check off our list of righteous deeds. Too often we come away with admirable scores on our church activity records, but with empty souls.

Moroni taught that good works which are done for the wrong reason (for praise of men, status, ego fulfillment, etc.) are not considered "righteousness" even though the very same deeds, when done in love and service would be.

> For behold, God hath said a man being evil cannot do that which is good; for if he offereth a gift, or prayeth unto God, except he shall do it with real intent it profiteth him nothing.
>
> For behold, it is not counted unto him for righteousness. (Moro. 7:6-7; see also verses 8-11.)

Somehow, the outward "works of the law," while essential to our growth, are insufficient in and of themselves to fill our souls with the spirituality that is found in the true righteousness of God. If we are not receiving peace and spiritual growth from our efforts in righteousness, then we are emphasizing the "works" part more than the "being" part. If our works are not bringing us toward Christ and Heavenly Father, they are empty, dead works.

There is no question that the righteousness of God includes "doing" along with "being." John warned that "whosoever doeth not righteousness is not of God" (1 Jn. 3:10). And, "he that doeth righteousness is righteous, even as he is righteous" (1 Jn. 3:7). Jesus said, "I will raise up unto myself a pure people that will serve me in righteousness" (D&C 58:27-28).

> For behold, the time is at hand that whosoever bringeth forth not good fruit, or *whosoever doeth not the works of righteousness,* the same [shall] have cause to wail and mourn (Alma 5:36).

The Savior is always concerned about what we do, but he is even more concerned about why we do it. The goal and purpose of all we do in the Church should be to become like him, and to help others come to him also. Thus it was that Alma taught that when men are judged and rewarded "according to their works," they will be judged not merely by what they have *done*, but also according to "that which they have *been*."

> . . . for the time is at hand that all men shall reap a reward of their works, *according to that which they have been. . .* (Alma 9:28).

Christ Is The Example And Source Of True Righteousness

Jesus set the awesome standard of true righteousness when he said, "I would that ye should be perfect even as I, or your Father who is in heaven is perfect" (3 Ne. 12:48).

> Therefore, what manner of men ought ye to be? Verily I say unto you, even as I am (3 Ne. 27:27; see also 3 Ne. 18:16).
>
> . . . wherefore, follow me, and do the things which ye have seen me do (2 Ne. 31:12; see also John 13:15).

Jesus came, not just to set a standard for the righteousness which we should seek in our lives, but also to demonstrate it. Throughout his life, he showed that the standard could be lived here on earth, even in the midst of evil. He came to show us exactly how we must live if we are to follow him. ". . . Christ also suffered for us, leaving us an example, that [we] should follow his steps" (1 Pet. 2:21).

> And now, my beloved brethren, I know by this that unless a man shall endure to the end, in following the example of the Son of the living God, he cannot be saved (2 Ne. 31:16; see also Morm. 7:10).

> But Israel, which followed after the law of righteousness, hath not attained to the law of righteousness.
>
> Wherefore? Because they sought it not by faith, but as it were by the works of the law. For they stumbled at the stumblingstone (Rom. 9:31-32).

Many in modern Israel continue to "stumble" over the simplicity of emulating the life of Christ. For some reason, we expect it to be more complicated than that. As we have said, it seems far easier to feel that we are "righteous" when we can simply go down our checklist of "good deeds" and score our performance. It is quite a different matter to exercise enough faith in Jesus Christ to enable us to draw upon his grace and power as we partake of his divine image and actually become like him. It is always harder "to be" than it is merely "to do."

> Then said they unto him, What shall we do, that we might work the [real and acceptable] works of God?
>
> Jesus answered and said unto them, *This is the work of God, that ye believe on him whom he hath sent.* (John 6:28-29.)

> For Moses describeth the righteousness which is of the law, That the man which doeth those things shall live by them.
>
> For Christ is the end of the law for righteousness to everyone that believeth. (Rom. 10:5, 4; see also Gal. 3:23-25; Deut. 6:24-25.)

When the scriptures say that Jesus is "the end of the law," they mean that he is the only example to follow. He is not just a GOOD example, he is THE example. As Truman Madsen said, "Here is an attempt to illustrate this magnificent Mormon insight: that Christ is both the revelation of God as he is and the revelation of man as he may become" (*Christ And The Inner Life,* S.L.C., Utah: Bookcraft, 1978, p. 1). The Apostle Peter said that we have been given, and that we will find in "the knowledge of him," everything we need to do and everything we need to become.

> According as his divine power hath given unto us *all things* that pertain unto life and godliness, *through the knowledge of him* that hath called us to glory and virtue (2 Pet. 1:3; see also D&C 93:19).

> The key to the door to the way of righteousness, then, is the knowledge of who and what Jesus Christ is . . .
>
> *Knowing what he is, we can know what the fullness of righteousness is.* Knowing what he did, we can see what we must do to become righteous as he is.
>
> *It follows that our whole spiritual endeavor should be focused on emulating the Master.* Mere external observance—church attendance, observing the laws of tithing, Word of Wisdom, and so on—are only the beginning; they do not fulfill the requirement.
>
> Though it is not easy, *we are required to so school ourselves to make habitual in our lives the kinds of response Jesus made to his life situations* and to act in keeping with such responses. To do this we will need to meet our own life situations and problems with questions such as: "How would Jesus feel?" and "What would Jesus do?" (1969-70 Gospel Doctrine Manual, *In His Footsteps Today,* S.L.C., Utah: Deseret Sunday School Union, 1969, pp. 5-7; emphasis added.)

The true righteousness which comes from knowing the Father through our knowledge and emulation of Jesus Christ is a gift of grace.

> For if by one man's offence death reigned by one; much more they which receive abundance of grace and of *the gift of righteousness* shall reign in life by one, Jesus Christ (Rom. 5:17).

> But unto every one of us is given grace according to the measure of the gift of Christ (Eph. 4:7).

Jesus, then, is not only the *example* and *standard* for what we are to become, he is also the *source* of grace and strength from which we may gain the power to become like him. ". . . their righteousness is of me, saith the Lord" (Isa. 54:17). "He shall receive the blessing from the Lord, and righteousness from the God of his salvation" (Ps. 24:5).

Such a fact presents a strange paradox. One might expect that before we could be acceptable to Diety, we would have to qualify by first becoming holy through our own good works. But the truth is that no one can become truly holy without God's help. It is the imitation righteousness of man that tries to be "good enough" for God with no dependence upon the atonement, nor acceptance of God's help in our quest. True righteousness requires the placing of our will and our obedience in submissive harmony with his divine will, so that he can work his miracles within us as he changes our nature (see Philip. 2:12-13).

> . . . This is the heritage of the servants of the Lord, and *their righteousness is of me,* saith the Lord (3 Ne. 22:17).
>
> Commit thy way unto the Lord; trust also in him; and *he shall bring it to pass.*
>
> And *he shall bring forth thy righteousness* as the light . . . (Ps. 37:5-6.)

It is pride which leads us to believe that Jesus wants and claims us because of our good works, but it was not because of how good we are that Jesus suffered and died for us. It was for precisely the opposite reason: He suffered and died for us because of how weak and sinful we are, and so that we could, through the power of his atonement, grow into godly perfection.

> *Not by works of righteousness which we have done,* but according to his mercy he saved us, by the washing of

> regeneration, and renewing of the Holy Ghost;
>
> Which he shed on us abundantly through Jesus Christ our Savior;
>
> *That being justified by his grace,* we should be made heirs according to the hope of eternal life. (Titus 3:5-7.)

The Power Of Righteousness

It is the integrity and the perfect holiness of God which gives him his power. It is not *who* God is that gives him his power throughout the universe, but *what* he is. The Lord made this relationship plain when he said, ". . . the devil was before Adam, for he rebelled against me, saying, Give me thine honor, which is my power. . ." (D&C 29:36). His honor is his power!

Man's checklist righteousness consisting only of good works, can never develop the personal power of character which comes by emulating the character of Christ. As we grow toward the image and likeness of Christ, we grow naturally toward the integrity and holiness which the Lord said gives him his power. We grow in his power as our lives become filled with a love of *who* he is and *what* he is. This is true righteousness (see Eph. 4:24). And, as we so order our lives, we gain power from him because we are becoming like him. The greater our personal honor and integrity, the greater will be our power over Satan, and over our own carnal nature.

> And because of the righteousness of his people, Satan has no power . . . for he hath no power over the hearts of the people, for they dwell in righteousness. . . (1 Ne. 22:26).

XIV
Patience

Webster's Seventh Collegiate Dictionary defines patience as the bearing of pains or trials calmly, without complaint; manifesting forbearance under provocation or strain, and being steadfast despite opposition, difficulty or adversity. Webster's Dictionary of Synonyms adds that "patience stresses calmness or composure, not only under suffering or under provocation, but also in awaiting an outcome that seems unduly or inordinately delayed, or in performing a task that makes severe demands upon one's attention." Other dictionaries add definitions such as, "to be undisturbed by obstacles, delays, or failures," and "to be persevering."

Patience is not a passive trait—it is an active dynamic virtue requiring the exercise of spiritual maturity, faith, hope, optimism, and trust. It is, as described by Neal A. Maxwell, "a willingness, in a sense, to watch the unfolding purposes of God with a sense of wonder and awe—rather than pacing up and down within the cell of our circumstance" (*Ensign*, October 1980, pp. 28-29). The scriptures contain hundreds of admonitions to acquire the virtue of patience. "But thou, O man of God . . . follow after . . . patience" (1 Tim. 6:11). ". . . be patient toward all men" (1 Thes. 5:14). "And now I would that ye should be . . . full of patience and longsuffering. . ." (Alma 7:23).

> For the natural man is an enemy to God, . . . unless he . . . becometh as a child, submissive, meek, humble, patient, full of love, willing to submit to all things which the Lord seeth fit to inflict upon him, even as a child doth submit to his Father (Mosiah 3:19).

The Example Of God's Patience

So characteristic is this kind attribute that Paul describes the Lord as "the God of patience" (Rom. 15:5). "The Lord is longsuffering, and of great mercy" (Num. 14:18). The scriptures emphasize that, as long as we are sincerely trying to obey him, the Lord will postpone his judgments and patiently use every means to strengthen our efforts as we try to follow the Savior's example. "Yea, and if it had not been for his matchless power, and his mercy, and his long-suffering toward us, we should unavoidably have been cut off from the face of the earth long before this period of time, and perhaps been consigned to a state of endless misery and woe" (Alma 9:11).

> The Lord is not slack concerning his promise, as some men count slackness; but is longsuffering to usward, not willing that any should perish, but that all should come to repentance (2 Pet. 3:9).
>
> But thou, O Lord, art a God full of compassion, and gracious, longsuffering, and plenteous in mercy and truth (Ps. 86:15).
>
> . . . I will be merciful unto them, saith the Lord God, if they will repent and come unto me; for mine arm is lengthened out all the day long, saith the Lord God of Hosts (2 Ne. 28:32; see also Alma 9:26).

The example of the Savior's patience with the cruel and unjustified insults and tortures inflicted upon him should motivate and strengthen our own patience. Let us "consider him that endured such contradiction of sinners against himself, lest [we] be wearied and faint in [our] minds" (Heb. 12:3).

Spiritual Practice and Exercise

> Ye must *practice* virtue and holiness before me continually (D&C 46:33).

Isaiah taught that orderly growth is accomplished here a little, and there a little, line upon line, precept upon precept (Isa. 28:10). Everything we see in nature teaches that there is an orderly process of growth and maturation. A spiritual harvest also requires time and patience.

Spiritual "practice" takes time. How foolish, then, to demand instant perfection from ourselves (or others) when the Lord does not. Since he is allowing us time to practice as we develop our righteousness before him, we should also allow ourselves time to overcome our faults without impatient self-condemnation along the way. "Ye are not able to abide the presence of God now, neither the ministering of angels; wherefore, continue in patience until ye are perfected" (D&C 67:13).

The strength of our commitment to "endure to the end" is often more important than the pace of our growth. Sometimes the hardest test of patience comes from expecting ourselves to grow toward perfection faster than our mortal limitations allow. Too often, as we attempt to "lengthen our stride," we confuse going fast with being valiant, when what is most needed is not speed but patient, steady growth. For "he that is hasty of spirit exalteth folly" (Prov. 14:29). This statement does not justify procrastination, but warns of the danger of falling prey to Satan's deception that we are unworthy simply because we cannot make ourselves perfect all at once.

The Lord understands that it takes time to change habits, and has counseled us to "be patient until [we] accomplish it" (D&C 11:19). As we develop spiritual maturity, we outgrow the "I-want-it-right-now" feelings, and learn to exercise the eternal perspective of patience which allows things to come to pass in their own time, according to the laws of nature and eternal progression.

> And see that all these things are done in wisdom and order; *for it is not requisite that a man should run faster than he has strength.* And again, it is expedient that he should be diligent, that thereby he might win the prize; therefore, *all things must be done in order.* (Mosiah 4:27.)
>
> Wherefore seeing we also are compassed about with so great a cloud of witnesses, let us lay aside every weight, and the sin which doth so easily beset us, and *let us run with patience the race that is set before us.*
>
> Looking unto Jesus the author and finisher of our faith; who for the joy that was set before him endured the cross. . . (Heb. 12:1-2.)

Being willing to "practice virtue and holiness" as we "run our race" with patience requires looking past the pains of our present circumstances, to view the rewards which lie ahead. However, the path which takes us closer to God is always cluttered with obstacles which we choose to call "trials and tribulations." Paul admitted what we already know, that "no chastening for the present seemeth to be joyous, but grievous." Nevertheless, he said, "afterward it yieldeth the peaceable fruit of righteousness *unto them which are exercised thereby*" (Heb. 12:11). The Greek translation for the word, "exercised," as used in this verse, is to be "trained and disciplined."

As we make our way through mortality, being "trained, disciplined and exercised" by the circumstances of life, we experience opposition and disappointments, for "the Lord seeth fit to chasten his people; yea, he trieth their patience and their faith" (Mosiah 23:21). As we encounter adversity we may respond with positive emotions such as trust, submissiveness and patience, or with negative emotions such as doubt and resentment—the "Why-is-God-doing-this-to-me?" attitude. Depending on the way we respond, we either grow stronger or weaker, as President Marion G. Romney described in the 1979-80 Melchizedek Priesthood manual:

> I have seen the remorse and despair in the lives of men who, in the hour of trial, have cursed God and died spiritually. And I have seen people rise to great heights from what seemed to be unbearable burdens.
>
> Finally, I have sought the Lord in my own extremities and learned for myself that my soul has made its greatest growth as I have been driven to my knees by adversity and affliction. (*He That Receiveth My Servants Receiveth Me,* pp. 24-25.)

> These things remain to overcome through patience, that such may receive a more exceeding and eternal weight of glory, otherwise, a greater condemnation (D&C 63:66).

Paul promised that all things work together for good to them that love God (see Rom. 8:28), but all things do not necessarily "work together for good" to those who refuse to be "exercised thereby," and who respond negatively and impatiently. When we allow ourselves to get tangled up in the seeming injustices of our trials, trying to blame God or someone else for the very situations which allow us to grow, we negate the benefits and experiences which the encounters were intended to provide. Our rebellious attitude plunges us into feelings of resentment and doubt. Not only do we fail the test and forfeit the growth, we also create barriers between us and God.

> I would exhort you to have patience, and that ye *bear with all manner of afflictions; that ye do not revile . . .*
>
> But that ye have patience, and bear with those afflictions, with a firm hope that ye shall one day rest from all your afflictions. (Alma 34:40-41.)

The Apostle James taught that we should "let patience have her perfect work, that [we] may be perfect and entire, wanting nothing" (James 1:4). And Alma promised that "whosoever shall put their trust in God shall be supported in their trials, and their troubles, and their afflictions. . ." (Alma 36:3). What an exciting promise the path of patience holds for those who allow it time to do its work! ("Let patience have her perfect work.")

There is a price to be paid for the blessings coming from spiritual patience. To gain those "peaceable fruits of righteousness," Paul said we must learn to actually "glory in tribulations," because "tribulation worketh [produces] patience," and "patience [produces] experience," which "experience [produces] hope: and hope maketh [us] not ashamed. . ." (Rom. 5:3-5).

We are told that "the trying of [our] faith worketh patience" (James 1:3), but Satan also uses our trials as opportunities to "whisper" discouragements about our unworthiness. It is important, therefore, to realize that many times the "trial of our patience" does not come from doing wrong, or even from our weaknesses, but rather, from our desires and efforts to do good. Special blessings are promised for patience under such conditions.

> For this is thankworthy, if a man for conscience toward God endure grief, suffering wrongfully.
>
> For what glory is it, if, when ye be buffeted for your faults, ye shall take it patiently? *but if, when ye do well, and suffer for it, ye take it patiently, this is acceptable with God.* (1 Pet. 2:19-20.)

> Now when our hearts were depressed, and we were about to turn back, behold, the Lord comforted us, and said. . . *bear with patience thine afflictions, and I will give unto you success* (Alma 26:27).

> . . . blessed is he that keepeth my commandments, whether in life or in death; *and he that is faithful in*

> *tribulation, the reward of the same is greater* in the kingdom of heaven (D&C 58:2).

Paul stated that we all "have need of patience, that, after ye have done the will of God, ye might receive the promise" (Heb. 10:36). Patience is willing to do what is right simply because it is right, without demanding an immediate reward, "for the people of the Lord are they who wait for him. . ." (2 Ne. 6:13).

> Be patient in afflictions, for thou shalt have many; but endure them, for lo, *I am with thee, even unto the end of thy days* (D&C 24:8).

Christ is aware of the suffering which comes from our spiritual "practice" and spiritual "exercise." To know that he understands our feelings and has promised to go with us through life's problems allows us to endure the trials of life with confidence and gratitude. When our self-image is rooted in the assurance of his love, and we are confident of his perfect justice, we can willingly and patiently accept anything that happens to us, and trust him to bring good out of it. We will be content to wait patiently for his hand to be revealed on our behalf, in his own way and in his own time. "Rest in the Lord, and wait patiently for him: fret not thyself. . ." (Psm. 37:7). Patience demonstates our trust. Impatience and "fretting" deny it.

> . . . the Lord did strengthen them that they could bear up their burdens with ease, and they did submit cheerfully and with patience to all the will of the Lord (Mosiah 24:15).

XV

Hope

No One Is Hopeless

When I reached the point of suicide, I was in utter despair. Wracked with guilt, I felt totally lost, hopeless, and helpless. Other words used to describe the depressing state of hopelessness are desperation, despondency, forlornness, dejection, melancholy, and gloom. These emotions can cause pain which is more severe and debilitating than the physical pain of a broken leg. Indeed, I am not aware of any other mental or emotional captivity so terrible.[10]

In some cases these emotions result from circumstances inflicted by Satan as he seeks to spread his misery, but in my case they came as the inescapable consequence of years of deliberate wickedness. As Moroni said, "And if ye have no hope ye must needs be in despair; and despair cometh because of iniquity" (Moro. 10:22). Of course, not all despair is the result of sin. Chemical imbalance in the brain cell chemistry can cause similar symptoms and is treatable

---

[10]See Alma 36:11-21 for a description of the agony of complete hopelessness and fear, as well as the joy of the transforming hope which is centered in Jesus Christ.

with non-addictive drugs.[11] Sin does, however, destroy hope because it brings alienation from God and prevents the confidence of hope. Satan would have us believe that such feelings are permanent and that there is no way out, but that is a lie. It is never too late to change; there is always hope for every person.

It is easy to understand why Satan works to magnify our problems. He knows the poisonous effect which despair has upon our service in the kingdom, upon our efforts to improve, and upon our ability to endure. He knows that a heart that is hurting from despair and hopelessness affects every part of our life. As we become negative and pessimistic, our mental and emotional energy drains away, leaving us empty and hollow, stripped of the will to fight back. Without hope we lose confidence that God even cares about us. We doubt his power and willingness to deliver us, and the powers of evil rejoice because they know that once we give up and separate ourselves from God, our spiritual progress is damned. "Hope deferred maketh the heart sick. . ." (Prov. 13:12).

Not even deliberate sin should cause a repentant person to give up hope of returning to harmony with God. Remember that "God sent not his Son into the world to condemn the world; but that the world through him might be saved" (John 3:17). It is my testimony that regardless of how deep our sins have been, no matter how long our sorrows have weighed us down, *no one*, except the Sons of Perdition, is beyond the power and grace of Jesus Christ. Other than this small, defiant group, no one has a problem too difficult for the Lord's redeeming grace. No one needs to be hopeless.

---

[11]For an excellent medical and scriptural discussion of the causes and cures of depression (in layman's terms) see: *Happiness Is A Choice* by Frank B. Minirth, M.D. and Paul D. Meier, M.D., Grand Rapids, Michigan, Baker Book House.

> And now, my beloved brethren, seeing that our merciful God has given us so great knowledge concerning these things, let us remember him, and lay aside our sins, and not hang down our heads, for we are not cast off . . . (2 Ne. 10:20).

We Are Saved By Hope

We cannot conquer our faults and find salvation from our sins without the power of hope, "for we are saved by hope. . ." (Rom. 8:24). ". . . wherefore man must hope, or he cannot receive an inheritance in the place which [God] has prepared" (Ether 12:32; see also Moro. 10:21). Dictionaries define hope as a strong desire which is fortified by a belief and expectation of its fulfillment. With this definition in mind, we would do well to ponder this question: Do I have a *real hope* of ever finding deliverance from the habits, fears, sins, and negative emotions which have been holding me back from being like Christ in my day-to-day life?

Our answer to that question is important because no one can rise to greater excellence without having hope—the belief and expectation—that they can do so. This being true, it becomes obvious that hope and faith are inseparable. "Wherefore, if a man have faith he must needs have hope: for without faith there cannot be any hope" (Moro. 7:42). "How is it that ye can attain unto faith, save ye shall have hope?" (Moro 7:40). "I would show unto the world that faith is things which are hoped for and not seen. . ." (Ether 12:6; see also Heb. 11:1).

It is not simply faith, however, which prepares us for life in the celestial kingdom, but faith *in Jesus Christ.* Sunlight passing through a magnifying glass gains no power until it is focused, and so it is with our faith. It is only when we focus our faith on Christ that we gain the hope and power to take us back to the Father. Only the true spiritual hope which is focused on Christ can enable us to *apply* our faith in conquest of our problems, and to look forward with "belief and expectation" to future achievements and blessings. Some, however, have mistaken spiritual hope for nothing more than a positive attitude. Consider, for example, the following entry in the memoirs of George A. Smith, dated in 1835, where he records what the Prophet Joseph Smith taught him about having a hopeful attitude.

> He told me I should never get discouraged whatever difficulties might surround me. If I was sunk in the lowest pit of Nova Scotia and all the Rocky Mountains piled on top of me, I ought not to be discouraged, but hang on, exercise faith and keep up good courage and I should come out on top of the heap. (Quoted in the 1976-77 Melchizedek Priesthood Manual, pp. 175-176.)

Such an attitude is commendable, but it is only a preliminary step toward the spiritual hope which holds the power of salvation. Those who desire to overcome deep-seated transgressions, to transform their weaknesses into strengths, to serve valiantly, and to grow closer to God need far more than a positive attitude to become Christlike.

The world offers many substitutes upon which we may focus our hope. It is full of psychological ideas for self-improvement and behavioral modifications. If such programs help us come closer to Christ, then we should embrace them. But we must use every caution against substituting the arm of flesh for hope and trust in the power of Christ and his gospel (see Moro. 7:13-17).

> And we desire that everyone of you do shew the same diligence *to the full assurance of hope* unto the end (Heb. 6:11).

> . . .lay hold upon the hope set before us:
>
> *Which hope we have as an anchor of the soul,* both sure and steadfast . . . (Heb. 6:18-19).

Why is hope in Christ so essential to our salvation?

Because it gives us the confidence to endure tribulations and obstacles that would otherwise defeat us. Without the sustaining power of hope, Satan can toss us about with the waves of temptations and the winds of doubt and confusion. But when we have the sure and steadfast anchor of hope, based upon knowledge and trust in God, we can travel through the frustrations of life with joy, gladness and confidence. Without hope, we simply could not persist.

> Wherefore, whoso believeth in God might with surety hope for a better world, yea, even a place at the right hand of God, which hope cometh of faith, [and] maketh an anchor to the souls of men, which would make them sure and steadfast, always abounding in good works, being led to glorify God (Ether 12:4).
>
> And thou shalt be secure, because there is hope. . . (Job 11:18).

How can we change our despairing emotions and hopeless attitudes to confidence, belief and expectation of success? We begin by repenting of the sins which have pulled us down to that "gulf of misery and endless wo" (Hel. 5:12). But what can we do if we have already tried to repent and have failed so many times that we no longer have any hope of repenting? The only way out of that dark chasm is through the power of Jesus Christ, for there is no hole too deep for him. We cannot fall beyond the reach of his love. The Savior has given us three sources of spiritual hope. One source is through the Holy Ghost, who gives the gift of hope to all those whose spirituality permits his companionship.

> . . . and because of meekness and lowliness of heart cometh the visitation of the Holy Ghost, *which Comforter filleth with hope*. . . (Moro. 8:26).
>
> Now the God of hope fill you with all joy and peace in believing, that ye may abound in hope, through the power of the Holy Ghost (Rom. 15:13).

Study of the scriptures also instills hope because that is where we gain gospel knowledge and learn of God's promises to help us live it.

> Wherefore, we search the prophets, and we have many revelations and the spirit of prophecy; *and having all these witnesses we obtain a hope,* and our faith becometh unshaken . . . (Jacob 4:6).
>
> For whatsoever things were written aforetime were written for our learning, *that we through patience and comfort of the scriptures might have hope* (Rom. 15:4).

Learning about Christ increases our faith and hope because it is in knowing him that we gain the confidence and trust which enables us to follow him back to the Father.

> Wherefore gird up the loins of your mind, be sober, and hope to the end for the grace that is to be brought unto you at the revelation (the revealing or unfolding) of Jesus Christ . . . (1 Pet. 1:13; see also Alma 58:11).

Thus, as we increase our comprehension of the goodness and power of Jesus Christ, as we come to know him personally, and as we experience him working in our life, we receive from him a growing dimension of confidence that we can rely upon him to help us fulfill all our needs.

We cannot continue to live in despair when we know that *no one* is beyond Christ's love, that he came into this world to rescue us from our sins, and that every person is of inestimable worth to him. "Casting all your care upon him; for he careth for you" (1 Pet. 5:7). What greater reason for hope?

When Jesus said, "I am able to make you holy. . ." (D&C 60:7), he was telling us that he knows how to help us discard the outward man of sin and weakness and give birth to the real person hidden within. Again, what greater reason could there be for hope?

Whatever it is we have been allowing to hold us back, we must let go of it now. Let us cast it aside for the treasure that can be ours through hope in the Savior. It is never too late.

> Blessed is the man that trusteth in the Lord, and whose hope the Lord is (Jer. 17:7).
>
> And what is it that ye shall hope for? Behold I say unto you that ye shall have hope through the atonement of Christ and the power of his resurrection, to be raised unto life eternal. . . (Moro. 7:41.)

XVI
The Master Physician

Admitting Our Need

Jesus Christ is the greatest physician who ever lived and healed upon this planet. Demoniacs, twisted and crippled limbs, blind eyes, deaf ears, palsy, leprosy—it mattered not, for there was no problem too great for the power of his tender touch of healing love. It mattered not whether he was approached by one or by multitudes, his healing power was granted to all who asked in faith. The Christ who walked the earth with compassion then is the same living Christ who serves the world in mercy today. He has not changed.

As great as his healings were, however, none are so awesome and precious as the touch of the Master's hand upon the sin-sick soul. Somehow the irresistible power of his stubborn love can reach into the heart and soul of a lost and despairing sinner and heal every wound. In some wonderful way he still works that miracle, transforming the wretched, empty shape of a sin-sick soul into a new creature, a beautiful child of God, born anew to the image of his Lord and Savior.

To enjoy physical, mental, and emotional health, we must live in harmony with the laws of God. On the other hand, whenever we try to cope with life or seek for happiness through any form of sin, we are not only in rebellion against

God, but we are also out of harmony with his laws of success. Consequently, we forfeit blessings and suffer from spiritual illness. The Lord uses the words, "sin" and "sickness" interchangeably.

> Behold, I came into the world not to call the righteous but *sinners* to repentance; the whole need no physician, but they that are *sick*. . . (Moro. 8:8).
>
> Return, ye backsliding children, and I will heal your backslidings (Jer. 3:22).

Sin, then, is not simply a transgression of God's laws, it is a symptom of spiritual sickness. Just as a fever or rash are symptoms indicating that something within our physical body is out of harmony with the laws of health, so also is sin a symptom that something within our spiritual life is out of harmony with the laws and purposes of God.

The Lord has warned that "the rebellious shall be pierced with much sorrow. . ." (D&C 1:3). Surely no torment can equal the pain and heartache which comes from a guilty conscience.

> . . . I fell upon my knees, and spread out my hands unto the Lord my God,
>
> And said, O my God, I am ashamed and blush to lift up my face to thee, my God: for our iniquities are increased over our head, and our trespass is grown up unto the heavens. (Ezra 9:5-6.)

As essential as repentance and conversion are to our spiritual progress, they are insufficient in and of themselves to heal us. Spiritual healing comes through our commitment, obedience, and forgiveness. No righteous person will ever find peace from their sins until they are reconciled to God.

> Conversion is effected by divine forgiveness, which remits sins. The sequence is something like this. He asks the

> Lord in prayer if it is true. The Holy Spirit gives him a witness. This is a testimony. If one's testimony is strong enough, he repents and obeys the commandments. By such obedience he receives divine forgiveness which remits sin. Thus he is converted to a newness of life. *His spirit is healed.* (Marion G. Romney: Conference Report, october 1963, p. 24; emphasis added).

Jesus Christ declared that one of the main purposes of his mission is to "heal the brokenhearted," bring "deliverance to the captives" who are held enslaved in spiritual bankruptcy by their sins, and "to set at liberty them that are bruised" by their battles with Satan and with their own carnal natures (Luke 4:18). No one can erase his own guilt or heal his own spiritual wounds. Only Christ, the Master Physician, can heal us of the spiritual sicknesses caused by sin. To him alone the Father gave the power and authority to reach inside our minds and hearts to work the miracle of spiritual healing.

> And Jesus went about . . . healing *all manner of sickness* and *all manner of disease* among the people.
>
> . . . and they brought unto him all sick people that were taken *with diverse diseases* and torments . . . and he healed them. (Matt. 4:23-24.)

> And he shall go forth, suffering *pains* and *afflictions* and temptations *of every kind;* and this that the word might be fulfilled which saith he will take upon him the pains and the sicknesses of his people.
>
> . . . and he will take upon him *their infirmities,* that his bowels may be filled with mercy, according to the flesh. . . (Alma 7:11-12.)

Notice how carefully the scriptures testify that Chris' has the power to heal "all manner" of sickness and disease infirmities, pains, and afflictions "of every kind," as well as the guilt, sorrow, discouragement, depression, and even despair which we suffer in consequence of sin.

The purpose of this chapter is not to suggest that the Lord has promised to heal every physical disease suffered by mankind. In his infinite wisdom, he often allows mortality to pursue its own course so that we may learn the lessons of life we came here to learn. Our purpose is, rather, to build confidence in accepting his invitation to come to him with our spiritual needs. “Come unto me, all ye that labour and are heavy laden, and I will give you rest” (Matt. 11:28).

Somehow, many of us have come to feel shame over the woes of our mortality, the very experiences we were sent here to encounter. What a regretable tragedy it is when we allow our hurts, our sins, our feelings, or any other forms of spiritual sickness to come between us and the Lord. What a tragedy when we have so little faith and trust in God that we dare not reveal our innermost frustrations and pains to him.

> Oh what peace we often forfeit;
> Oh what pain we needless bear,
> All because we do not carry
> Everything to God in prayer.
>
> (Author Unknown)

When we have an infection or disease in our body, we do not feel ashamed to go to medical doctors for help, so why should we feel ashamed to admit to God that we need his spiritual help? We go for medical help because we have a medical problem and because we have faith in the doctor’s ability to cure us. Why, then, when we have spiritual problems, are we reluctant to go to the greatest Physician of all? The medical doctor does not “look down” on us for having a problem. Rather, he is delighted with the opportunity to serve by restoring our health. He respects us for caring enough about our health to take the appropriate action. Will God respect us less for coming to him for help?

> Come unto me, all ye that labour and are heavy laden, and I will give you rest (Matt. 11:28).

By His Stripes We Are Healed

The Savior's power to heal our spiritual needs rests within the effects of the atonement. The concept expressed in Isaiah 53:5 that we are "healed by his stripes" is very personal and sacred to me, for it was by learning how the Savior's atonement applied to my own sins that I was freed from the guilt and despair in which I had planned my suicide, and my life was changed.

I must tell you that I still do not understand the miracle by which he healed me of my sins and replaced my guilt and failure with victory, forgiveness, peace, and love. I can find no words to explain it. There are, however, some key scriptures which, when prayerfully pondered, will guide one to a further understanding.

> Wherefore, we would to God that . . . all men would believe in Christ, and view his death, and suffer his cross and bear the shame of the world (Jacob 1:8).

What did Jacob mean by "viewing his death"? What did he mean when he said that we should partake of the suffering which Jesus endured upon the cross, and that we should recognize and bear our part of the world's shame for His suffering? The Savior commanded us to "take up [our] cross daily" as we follow him (Luke 9:23). He also commanded us to "look unto me in every thought . . . [and to] behold the wounds which pierced my side, and also the prints of the nails in my hands and feet. . ." (D&C 6:36-37). How can we view and understand these things which took place so long ago? How can *we* partake of *his* suffering? Why is this awareness so important that we must attend to it daily? And finally, what does all this have to do with our spiritual healing?

When the scriptures command us to "view" these things, it means that we are to mentally and emotionally place ourselves there in Gethsemane so that we can visualize his agonizing ordeal. His suffering should become so real that we can actually see the blood oozing from every pore of his tortured body and know that it was done because of our sin. It means that we should try to hear and feel his groans of agony as he took upon himself the effects of our own sins—our pain, our guilt and shame, our punishments *the same as if he had committed the sins himself.*

We should also be able to "view" his sufferings on the cross with such reality that we can imagine the splinters of the rough wood piercing his quivering flesh as he is cruelly thrust down upon the cross, his back still raw from the Roman scourging. We should hear the sound of the mallet as it drove those rough, rusty nails through the flesh of his weary hands and feet. The Savior's sacrifice should become so real and vivid to us that we are able to see and hear the agonizing tearing of his sacred flesh as the heavy cross is lifted, then cruelly dropped into the hole with a heartrending thud. We need to literally and vividly "view his death" and "behold the wounds" as he hung there, exhausted, misunderstood, hated, and rejected of men.

Paul understood and emphasized the importance of this vicarious visualization. "For I determined not to know anything among you, save Jesus Christ, and him crucified" (1 Cor. 2:2). ". . . I die daily" (1 Cor. 15:31), "always bearing about in the body the dying of the Lord Jesus, that the life also of Jesus might be made manifest in our body" (2 Cor. 4:10).

> I am crucified with Christ: nevertheless I live; yet not I, but Christ liveth in me: and the life which I now live in the flesh I live by the faith of the Son of God, who loved me, and gave himself for me (Gal. 2:20).

Isaiah also helps us to share in our part of the Savior's burdens, and to internalize the personal implications of the atonement.

> Surely he hath borne our griefs, and carried our sorrows: yet we did esteem him stricken, smitten of God, and afflicted.
>
> But he was wounded for our transgressions, he was bruised for our iniquities: the chastisement of our peace was upon him; and with his stripes we are healed. (Isa. 53:4-5.)

How can we "suffer his cross" and "view his death" and "bear [our part of] the shame of the world" without weeping in remorse knowing that he did it all both for us and because of us? It was not "for the sins of the world" that Jesus suffered and died; it was not for "them," not for "us," not even for "all of mankind;" it was for EACH of mankind. The Savior not only suffered for each person, but also because of each person. "For Christ also hath once suffered for sins, the just for the unjust, that he might bring us to God. . ." (1 Pet. 3:18).

When the anguish of our guilt crushed down upon him and he "fell on his face" (Matt. 26:39) "being in an agony" (Luke 22:44), and when he shrank in horror from the new and unfamiliar feelings of guilt and shame (D&C 19:18), feelings which crushed down upon him so heavily that he sweat "great drops of blood" (Luke 22:44), he was suffering the punishment for each person's individual sins. I believe that in some way which is incomprehensible to us, the Savior looked forward from Gethsemane, and backward through the corridors of time and then, person by person, sin by sin, paid a price for us which was infinite in its totality, but *finite and specific* in its detailed pain.

> . . . for behold, he suffereth *the pains of all men, yea, the pains of every living creature,* both men, women, and children, who belong to the family of Adam (2 Ne. 9:21).

> The suffering he undertook to endure, and which he did endure, *equaled the combined suffering of all men* (Marion G. Romney, quoted in the 1974-75 Melchizedek Priesthood Manual, p. 47; emphasis added).

"We love him, because he first loved us" (1 Jn. 4:19). And "hereby perceive we the love of God, because he laid down his life for us. . ." (1 Jn. 3:16). It is in "perceiving" his infinite sorrow and pain for each of us that we glimpse the magnitude of his perfect love. "I think of his hands pierced and bleeding to pay the debt! Such mercy, such love, and devotion can I forget?" (Hymns No. 80.) As the reality of the kindness and love of his sacrifice are spiritually perceived, our proud hearts are broken and the door is opened to receive his healing influence. What can make our spirits more "contrite" than to walk back through the corridors of our own memory, reviewing each sinful act which added to his pain, and then asking Heavenly Father to "apply the atoning blood of Christ that we may receive forgiveness of our sins, and [that] our hearts may be purified. . ."? (Mosiah 4:2).

We are "healed by his stripes" because the spiritual awareness that his suffering was not only for us, but also because of us, creates a devotion to him which is so firm that we resolve to never again add to his pain with another deliberate sinful act. We are "healed by his stripes" because this understanding causes our hearts to burst with a deep love and appreciation for him. And, in coming to feel the enormity of our debt, we are born anew into a spiritual union with him that can be found in no other way.

> For the preaching [and viewing and bearing] of the cross is to them that perish foolishness; but unto us which are saved it is the power of God (1 Cor. 1:18).

> For as the sufferings of Christ abound in us, so our consolation also aboundeth by Christ.

> . . . as ye are partakers of the sufferings, so shall ye be also of the consolation (2 Cor. 1:5, 7).

> My son, be faithful in Christ . . . and may his sufferings and death . . . rest in your mind forever (Moro. 9:25).

All The Way Or Nothing

When the Savior acts as our spiritual physician, the resulting healing will be perfect, even if it is only from the touch of faith.

> . . . and as many as touched were made *perfectly whole.* (Matt. 14:36).

In order to receive the perfect healing influence of his grace we must be willing to go further into our problems than a mere surface treatment of the outward symptoms. God never intended life to be comfortable, but rather, he commanded us to strive toward perfection (Matt. 5:48). We may come to him seeking only the release of our pain, but he will settle for nothing less than the removal of its cause. (How often we ask the Lord to change everything—but us.) It is not his way to treat the outward symptoms. Our perfect joy and fulfillment—that is what he is most interested in.

Doctor William Parker relates a case which demonstrates the difficulty of seeking Christ's healing influence when we are not ready or willing to "go all the way" with him, but are only seeking the relief of a surface treatment.

> To surrender now, this minute, we not only offer our lives, our virtues, talents, will, but our burdens and demons (such as shame, fear, hurts, hate, etc.) as well. These latter will dissolve in proportion to our willingness to be made whole. Most of us think we are already willing to be made whole (healed). But are we?

A woman of forty, a housewife and mother, entered Prayer Therapy when the physicians as well as her spiritual advisor had given up all hope of helping her to overcome alcoholism. She wanted desperately to stop drinking, was carrying a load of guilt, fear, shame that had driven her twice to unsuccessful attempts to end her life. Her slips (test results) revealed deep seated resentments, tremendous self-pity, guilt, inferiority, a staggering burden separating her from any awareness of Love's healing power. Deeply religious, she could not understand why her prayers to stop drinking had not been answered.

At first she showed little interest in eliminating the detrimental personality aspects uncovered to her. "I want to stop drinking first," she repeated. "If I can't stop that, what does it matter? Why doesn't God help me?"

God couldn't help her because she wouldn't let Him. She was not willing to let go and let God. She began to realize this when we studied a healing recorded in St. John which contained a puzzling question by Jesus. *He asked a man who had been infirm for thirty-eight years, "Wilt thou be made whole?"*

Now, as we have agreed, almost everyone suffering to any degree believes they are willing to be made whole. Still, Jesus must have had something specific in mind. Isn't what most of us want to be healthy, or free of pain, or free of debt, just as the one thing our alcoholic wanted was to stop drinking?

When the purport of Jesus' question dawned on her she found that, in her heart of hearts, *she had not been willing to be made whole—only sober.* She wished the pain of drink (only a symptom in reality) removed whilest she clung to her resentments, her self-pity, her guilts and so forth. This cannot be. We must be willing to surrender everything.

Unless a person is psychotic, the ego within each of us has the upper hand. This often makes it difficult for us to surrender our detrimental feelings and attitudes. We have to learn to surrender ourselves—our whole world of inner feeling—to a Spirit greater than our own. True prayer means releasing ourselves under the compulsion of the highest, not in dreary resignation, but in joy and trust. (William R. Parker & Elaine St. Johns, *Prayer Can Change Your Life,* 17th Ed.,

> Englewood Cliffs, N.J.: Prentice-Hall, Inc., 1965, pp. 124-125; emphasis added.)

C. S. Lewis emphasized the same theme, that Christ, being perfect, and wanting to help us enjoy the victory of perfection, will not settle for less. Either he works with us on his terms or not at all. He is in charge; he sets the standards for righteousness, which is no less than being "made perfectly whole" (Matt. 14:36).

> . . . He never talked vague, idealistic gas. When He said, "Be perfect," he meant it. *He meant that we must go in for the full treatment.* It is hard; but the sort of compromise we are all hankering after is harder—in fact it is impossible. It may be hard for an egg to turn into a bird: it would be a jolly sight harder for it to learn to fly while remaining an egg. We are like eggs at present. And you cannot go on indefinitely being just an ordinary, decent egg. We must be hatched or go bad.
>
> I find a good many people have been bothered by what I said in the last chapter about Our Lord's words, "Be ye perfect." Some people seem to think this means "Unless you are perfect, I will not help you;" and as we cannot be perfect, then, if He meant that, our position is hopeless. But I do not think He did mean that. I think He meant *"The only help I will give is help to become perfect. You may want something less: but I will give you nothing less."*
>
> Dozens of people go to Him to be cured of some one particular sin which they are ashamed of . . . (and) . . . which is obviously spoiling daily life. Well, He will cure it all right: but He will not stop there. *That may be all you asked; but if once you call Him in, He will give you the full treatment.*
>
> "Make no mistake," He says, "if you let me, I will make you perfect. The moment you put yourself in My hands, that is what you are in for. Nothing less, or other, than that. *You have free will, and if you choose, you can push Me away. But if you do not push Me away, understand that I am going to see this job through.* Whatever suffering it may cost you in your earthly life, whatever inconceivable purification it may cost you after death, *whatever it costs Me, I will never rest, nor let you rest, until you are literally perfect—until My*

Father can say without reservation that He is well pleased with you, as He said He was well pleased with Me. This I can do and will do. But I will not do anything less."

And yet—this is the other and equally important side of it—this Helper who will, in the long run, be satisfied with nothing less than absolute perfection, will also be delighted with the first feeble, stumbling effort you make tomorrow to do the simplest duty. (C. S. Lewis, *Mere Christianity,* 29th Ed., N.Y., N.Y.: MacMillan Publishing Co., Inc., 1979, pp. 169-172; emphasis added. Compare Philip. 1:6.)

Epilogue

Before we part company I want to briefly summarize my feelings. At the beginning of the book I described the confusion I felt when the Savior applied his grace in my life as he helped me make changes I had been unable to accomplish, and as he opened my eyes to the real power of the Gospel. I also asked you to set aside any resentments or failures which might have been causing barriers between you and the Lord, long enough to explore these pages with me. We have come a long way together since those preliminary remarks, but I cannot end our time together without sharing a final testimony that the principles we have discussed are true. I know they carry the power to change lives, for I have experienced their effect in my own life, and I have seen them work in the lives of many others who have also gained victory over difficult problems in their lives.

I take no credit for the things presented in this book, for I have recorded only what I learned as the Savior came into my life and changed my nature from carnal darkness and doubt to spiritual victory and freedom. I do not expect anyone to accept these ideas based upon my word alone, but I have tried to demonstrate the truth of every principle with scripture and quotations from Church leaders, Sunday

School and Priesthood manuals. More important, however, than those documentations, is the promised witness of the Holy Ghost to every person who seeks "with real intent" (Moro. 10:4-5). It is important for us to rely upon that witness of the truth, and also to draw upon the same inspiration as we learn how to *apply* these truths in our efforts to live the gospel.

At the end of a fireside where I had described the changes the Savior brought into my life, I was asked if the change in my nature was instantaneous, or if it was a gradual process. My answer to both questions was yes. Yes, there was an instant change, a surprising peace, power, and confidence which came into my being from the moment I finally stopped trying to be my own savior and surrendered instead to Christ. But there was also a natural process of orderly growth which was required to make those changes in my character permanent.

It only takes a split second to commit our lives to God, but it requires time to live that commitment. It takes time and patience to learn and understand his will, time to repent, time to grow and conquer weaknesses and change habits. It takes time to perfect ourselves as we seek to emulate the Master, and that exciting adventure of eternal progression will occupy us throughout the eternities.

The point of that question is important: how long does it take to become free? It is my testimony that we can turn and walk away from our bad habits and sins, even from addictions and compulsions, and, through the power of Christ, obtain victory from the *very moment* we put him first in our life. Of course, we will continue to struggle as we seek to make those changes permanent. No one needs to live with evil and enslaving habits because Jesus Christ stands ready to fill the "gaps" as we do all we can, and then trust in his grace to help us go the rest of the way. What an exciting partnership! "Greater is he that is in you, than he that is in the world" (1 Jn. 4:4).

There is one scripture which is probably quoted more often than any other. It is: "For God so loved the world, that he gave his only begotten Son, that whosoever believeth in him should not perish, but have everlasting life" (John 3:16). I must confess that I used to marvel over the emotion displayed by some who quoted this beautiful verse. Because I took the Savior's life and suffering for granted, it was a mystery to me why this verse moved people so much. It is no longer a mystery.

Many, however, continue to doubt God's love for them because, without their realizing it, Satan has convinced them that God's love is conditioned upon our "goodness" or "badness." While this feeling is common, it is entirely untrue, for God's perfect love is completely unconditional. While it is true that our sins may alter our ability to feel his love, there is nothing we can do to diminish it. "Behold, he sendeth an invitation unto all men, for the arms of mercy are extended towards them, and he saith: Repent, and I will receive you" (Alma 5:33). ". . . and he inviteth them all to come unto him and partake of his goodness; and he denieth none that come unto him. . ." (2 Ne. 26:33).

> Behold, hath the Lord commanded any that they should not partake of his goodness? Behold I say unto you, Nay; but *all men are privileged the one like unto the other,* and none are forbidden. (2 Ne. 26:28).

> . . . for the Lord your God is gracious and merciful, *and will not turn away his face from you,* if ye return unto him (2 Chr. 30:9).

When the Savior told us that not even a lowly sparrow can fall without his notice, and that even the hairs on our head are numbered, he was indicating the depth of his personal love and concern for each person (see Matt. 10:29-31). For years I have searched for words to describe the magnitude of that overwhelming love which I felt as the power of Christ came into my life. But I have learned that mortal man is utterly incapable of describing something so vast, so infinite and all-encompassing, yet so intimate, pure, and individual.

Paul said that "the love of Christ . . . passeth knowledge" (Eph. 3:19). To me, this means that his love is so great, so pure and so far above anything we can presently comprehend, that it cannot be described, understood, or perceived by mere study or learning. And yet, even knowing this, Paul prayed that we might come to "know the love of Christ, which passeth knowledge . . ." (Eph. 3:19). If the love of God passes beyond the capability of our knowledge and understanding, then how can it be known? Only by personal experience; only by feeling it in our hearts rather than analyzing it with our minds.

The Savior promised that he will "draw near" to every person who draws near to him (see D&C 88:63; 6:20; 3 Ne. 9:14; Alma 26:15; 2 Ne. 1:15). He never said, "If you try to draw near to me, then I will receive you when you finally get here." He never intended to be only our destination, but also, to be our companion and guide along the way. He will patiently, tenderly lead us through all we need to experience as we prepare to return to the Father. As we turn away from the world, as we let go of all our substitutes and take those first timid steps toward the Savior, we will always discover him there, leaning forward with his loving arms stretched toward us, just as a parent reaches toward its child when it is learning to walk.

Much of the sorrow we have experienced came from the mistaken belief that no one understood or cared what we were going through—that we were alone in our sufferings. But the scriptures reveal that when the millennium begins, and we finally understand just how close and involved the Lord has been in our daily lives, we will be so awed that we "shall mention the loving kindness of [our] Lord, and all that he has bestowed upon [us] according to his goodness and according to his loving kindness, forever and ever, [and that] in all [our] afflictions he was afflicted." (D&C 133:52-53; compare Isaiah 63:7-9.)

When we fail to receive comfort in the midst of our trials and sorrows, the fault always lies within ourselves, and not with God, for "ye may know of a surety that I, the Lord God, do visit my people in their afflictions" (Mosiah 24:14).

> Can a woman forget her sucking child, that she should not have compassion on the son of her womb? Yea, they may forget, *yet will I not forget thee.* (Isa. 49:15.)
>
> Blessed be God, even the Father of our Lord Jesus Christ, the Father of mercies, and *the God of all comfort;*
> Who comforteth us in all our tribulation . . . (2 Cor. 1:3-4.)

Without a knowledge of God's love and goodness, the experiences of life can make us hard, cold, and bitter. But when we find his power and love manifest in our struggles, we feel compelled to respond with an increase of love and devotion toward him. We yearn to be worthy of him, to become more like him, and to share him with the ones we love.

May you find here not the end of a book, but the beginning of a new life, an exciting journey, a closer and more victorious walk with God, "which always causeth us to triumph in Christ. . ." (2 Cor. 2:14).

> What you sincerely in your heart think of Christ will determine what you are, will largely determine what your acts

will be. No person can study this divine personality, can accept his teachings without becoming conscious of an uplifting and refining influence with himself. (David O. McKay, *Gospel Ideals,* 7th Abridged Edition, S.L.C., Utah: Improvement Era Publication, 1953, p. 34.)

Who shall separate us from the love of Christ? Shall tribulation, or distress, or persecution, or famine, or nakedness, or peril, or sword?

Nay, in all these things we are more than conquerors through him that loved us. (Rom. 8:35, 37.)

On those days when earthly friends may disappoint you, remember that the Savior of all mankind has described Himself as your friend. He is your very best friend. (Spencer W. Kimball, The New Era, July 1980, p. 10.)

You May contact the author by writing to:

Steven Carmer
P.O. Box 60204
Phoenix, Arizona 85082

Topical Index